BROKENOMICS

50 WAYS TO LIVE THE DREAM ON A DIME

DINA GACHMAN

SEAL PRESS

BROKENOMICS
50 Ways to Live the Dream on a Dime

Library of Congress Cataloging-in-Publication Data

Gachman, Dina.
Brokenomics : 50 ways to live the dream on a dime / Dina Gachman.
pages cm
ISBN 978-1-58005-567-3 (pbk.)
1. Budgets, Personal. 2. Finance, Personal. 3. Cost and standard of living.
I. Title.
 HG179.G2342 2015
 332.024—dc23
 2014035697

Published by
Seal Press
A Member of the Perseus Books Group
1700 Fourth Street
Berkeley, California
Sealpress.com

Cover design by Kate Basart
Printed in the United States of America
Distributed by Publishers Group West

9 8 7 6 5 4 3 2 1

For Mom, Dad, Amy, Jackie, and Kathryn

And for JZ (the original)

CONTENTS

VII. WORK

VIII. LOVE AND RELATIONSHIPS

Introduction

WELCOME TO BROKENOMICS

I n the classic Preston Sturges movie *Sullivan's Travels*, a well-to-do film director named John L. Sullivan gets fed up with making comedies and decides to take on an important, serious picture about human suffering. He has no clue how normal people function since he's been living the high life of three-martini lunches, five-star dinners, and country-club tennis courts and swimming pools, so in an effort to understand the material, he goes undercover as a hobo so he can experience what it's like to . . . be a hobo.

Sullivan hits up the studio costume department and trades in his high-waisted designer suit for some pretend hobo duds and a bindle attached to a stick. He then sloughs off his distinguished appellation in favor of the more down-and-out sounding nickname "Sully" and sets out to learn what makes the little people tick. Sully enters the big, bad world with ten cents in his pocket and declares: "I'm not coming back until I know what trouble is!" At a diner, he meets a broke aspiring actress wearing a very swanky evening gown who's been booted out of her apartment. She's referred to as "The Girl," and she's played by Veronica Lake, who is just about the most gorgeous pauper you've ever seen. "I haven't got a yacht or a pearl necklace or a country seat or even a window seat," The Girl tells Sully. Soon enough he agrees to let her come along on his little adventure, and The Girl gets outfitted in some "tramp" clothes of her own.

What Sully discovers along the way—besides the fact that The Girl has more street smarts than he does—is that in tough times, people don't want to watch movies about human suffering. They just want to laugh at cartoons and chew some tobacco. "It isn't much, but it's better than nothing in this cockeyed caravan," says Sullivan, who by that point is world-weary from weeks of living off canned beans and stale coffee.

In Sully's day they had the Rockefellers, Coco Chanel's Bijoux de Diamants jewelry collection, and Hearst Castle. Now, almost a century later, we have superyachts, bespoke submarines, pop stars building floating mansions in Greece, six-dollar coffee drinks, and ten-dollar pressed juice, so it's safe to say that we're living in a cockeyed caravan of our own. I'm not implying that you're a hobo because you're reading a book called *Brokenomics*. But, compared to people who can afford caviar facials and $80,000 African safaris, we're all maybe, possibly, just a bit hobo-*esque*.

Not that the hobo-esque life doesn't have its merits. I imagine the upkeep on a floating mansion would cost a fortune, and if I'm ever within a ten-foot radius of caviar I'd like to shove it into my piehole and eat it, not waste it by putting it on my face. That's just common sense. This, my friends, is Brokenomics: a practical, real-world approach to finance that's all about living the high life—whether you're making peanuts or pulling in six figures. The point is to have fun while you're working toward six figures even if you're still at the peanut stage. It's also about cultivating a healthy attitude when it comes to money. Do you overspend on fancy creams made with orchid essence and green bean extract? Brokenomics can help. Do you think that spending $300 a year on lotto tickets will solve all your problems? Stick around. Does the thought of talking about money with your husband, wife, lover, or partner cause you to break out in hives, sweat profusely, and start pounding whiskey shots or two-for-one bottles of rosé? You're not alone.

Right about now you might be wondering what sort of credentials I possess that make me such a sage financial guru. For better or worse (I'm thinking better), I do not have perfectly coiffed hair, spectacular muscle tone, billions of dollars, or really white teeth. Despite all that, I do know for a fact that there is no surefire way to "get rich quick" unless you rob Richard Branson or elope with Sara Blakely, the billionaire creator of Spanx—without a prenup of course. You have a better chance of getting rich quick by eating a spoonful of black-eyed peas on New Year's Day (a Southern tradition that promises prosperity and luck that I always observe just in case) than you do by walking on hot coals, joining a multilevel marketing "opportunity," or spending thousands of dollars on weekend seminars with names like XTREME MAX MONEY MIRACLE. At least black-eyed peas are cheap, full of fiber, and delicious. You do the math.

What I do have are experiences, and those experiences have not always been glorious. At times they have been mortifying, humiliating, demoralizing, and ridiculous—but they have all been educational. I know, for example, how to save enough money to travel: by sleeping on a friend's couch for months and working at a restaurant so divey it's been unofficially nicknamed Seagull Feather Heaven (more on that in chapter 23). I have weighed the financial implications of having a child versus raising a nice potted plant. (While the jury's still out on this one, the plant is obviously much less pricey and much more docile.) I have fixed my car with Velcro and hemmed my pants with a stapler. I've faced my student loans head-on, even though there've been many moments when I considered changing my identity and moving into a nondescript hut on the outskirts of Guadalajara to escape the clutches of that demon succubus Sallie Mae. I've also learned that screaming at the Sallie Mae customer service people will not make your loans go away. Please see chapter 40 for more juicy details on that one.

I don't mean to be a Debbie Downer, but Oprah is not going to slide down your chimney, bop you on the head with her magical Tory Burch wand, and get you the promotion that will catapult you into her tax bracket. Any promotion you do get will happen because you earned it, you asked for it, and you have a boss who is a fair human being—not a robotic, micromanaging, bottom-line-obsessed d-bag who thinks your name is Productivity Enhancer, not Betty Jones or Bob Horton or whatever. (If you've spent any time at all waiting tables or slouching toward retirement in a cubicle, you know this type of moniker mix-up can sometimes happen.)

Unless you actually are living off the grid in a burlap teepee, finances impact every aspect of your life: love, education, where you sit at concerts, when you board a plane, where you live, and how you feel about math. Rest assured, you do not have to be good at math to be smart about money. You just have to be able to tolerate math, which, depending on how your brain works, is not always as easy-breezy as it sounds.

Now, there are plenty of dead-serious self-help manifestos out there that promise to make you rich, skinny, successful, and fulfilled. Think of Brokenomics as a financial call to arms with a sense of humor. A comedic economic manifesto for the masses! It's not about feeling mopey because you can't afford a private jet with solid gold fuselage. We'd all love free-flowing Dom Pérignon and an infinity pool, and some of you may even covet an infinity pool filled with Dom Pérignon, but it's not about that. It's about surviving and thriving, no matter what your situation might be. I don't need a ball gown made of pulverized diamonds, and I bet you don't either. Besides: how many times have you stood all primped-up at a fancy event and thought: "I can't wait to get out of here, jump back into jeans, and meet my friends for happy hour." I'm guessing your answer falls somewhere between "two" and "fifteen," depending on variables like age, attitude, rank, and access to highbrow events. However many fancy events you attend, we're all in this cockeyed caravan together—so let's make the most of it.

I.

PHILOSOPHIES

Capital as such is not evil; it is its wrong use that is evil.
Capital in some form or other will always be needed.
—Gandhi

I've never been a millionaire, but I just know I'd be darling at it.
—Dorothy Parker

1

THERE WILL ALWAYS BE SOMEONE RICHER, TALLER, SMARTER, AND BETTER LOOKING THAN YOU

Brokenomics is all about tough (yet everlasting) love, so let's just start off with a few basic truths. Like the fact that your finances are 100 percent your responsibility—unless you were robbed blind by the world's cleverest cat burglars, who wiped out your entire bank account and took all your possessions before disappearing into thin air. Chances are this hasn't happened to you, and if it has, that's what the FBI is for, so let's just move ahead.

Say you've done everything right: you studied hard, got a degree, created the world's most irresistible résumé, and landed an entry-level dream job that pays peanuts but it's a paycheck and you get medical and dental and a little magnetic swipey card that grants you access to the parking garage. You're feeling pretty proud of yourself so you decide to celebrate—good for you! Then let's say that celebration includes a pair of Louboutins and a six-course prix fixe dinner for five of your closest friends.

This behavior is:

A. Questionable, but understandable

B. Totally cool because you can put it all on your credit card

C. Psychotic

D. Irresponsible as hell

E. Both C & D

If you answered B, we have a long way to go, but that's OK. If your answer is C, I like your passion. But the correct answer, according to the Laws of Brokenomics, is D. Irresponsible as hell. Answering E or C isn't necessarily wrong, but it's a little judgy, and we're not here to judge. It's very generous that you want to treat your friends to a fancy dinner, but if that's out of your budget range, you could instead treat them to a round at happy hour (still a little pricey, depending on how many people show up); make them cookies (cheap yet thoughtful); or just verbally tell them how much you love them, which is free yet still sweet. If they expect you to lavish them with gifts, you might need to look into making new friends.

I'm all about having fun. Happy hour is a wonderful time of day, and it's definitely not a party if you're sitting at home, staring at the stains in your popcorn ceiling, and hoarding money in your mattress. When taking responsibility for your finances, it's important to learn when to splurge and when to save. So let's examine another scenario.

You've just finished your fellowship year and you're now a colorectal surgeon—you're getting *paid*! You:

A. Immediately purchase a starter yacht, which you will never be able to use because you're a busy surgeon

B. Pledge to never go out and to only eat canned peas and Melba toast so you can save up the millions you'll need to really enjoy life when you're in your eighties and rocking Depends

C. Take a close look at your finances, calculate whether you can finally afford that Mazda and get rid of the beat-up Pinto you inherited from your grandfather, realize it's in your budget range and buy the Mazda, and then drive around town blaring Shakira

D. Google to see if the Taylor-Burton diamond is for sale

I'm guessing that you're a smart or at least smart-ish person, so hopefully you chose C, since it's the right answer. Being so frugal that you don't enjoy life and you only eat Melba toast is almost as irresponsible as blowing your paycheck on a yacht. If you're going to eat the same thing every day, at least make it something delicious yet affordable. It's about balance. Sometimes things happen in life—you get laid-off; your deranged sociopath of a landlord raises your rent; your tuition spikes; your cable company sends a letter declaring you've been "enjoying a discounted rate" for the last four years and they're suddenly jacking up the price because you are powerless and they are assholes. These infuriating scenarios are the reason that things like anger management classes and yoga retreats exist, but, in order to progress to the next stage of Brokenomics, you need to immediately pledge that you are the only one responsible for your finances. Do it right this second. You are the master of your fate. You can also do it later on today or even tomorrow. Whenever you're ready.

> *Being so frugal that you don't enjoy life and you only eat Melba toast is almost as irresponsible as blowing your paycheck on a yacht.*

Needing to take responsibility in life starts much earlier than many of us would like, whether that means responsibility for our decisions about school, friendship, love, or money. It also means taking responsibility for the way we process and learn from obstacles, tough breaks, or financial challenges. One of the first lessons I learned about handling setbacks happened way back in elementary school, when my mom shared some age-old wisdom that has stayed with me into adulthood, although it took several years for me to appreciate what she was saying since I spent a good portion of my early years dismissing every word that came out of her mouth as the out-of-touch ramblings of a suburban lunatic. It all started, like many life lessons, on the playground.

It was fifth grade, and I had fallen madly in love with Ray Espinoza. I didn't understand love then, but he looked good to me, and neurons and protons and whatever else were ping-ponging around in my cells every time he tied his shoe or kicked some dirt, so it was pretty clearly the real deal. One day, in a burst of passion, I decided to pledge my love via index card. Ray was beautiful—he wore tube socks and polyester shorts during recess. He was great at soccer—at least, from what I could tell. When you add all of that together, it's easy to see that this was a guy who was very worthy of a daring, poetic gesture.

And so, that very night I hid in my bedroom closet with a stack of index cards. Wielding a blue marker, I mustered all my courage, summoned the muses, and wrote: I LIKE YOU. FROM DINA. The next day I carried the heartfelt ode around in the pocket of my disco-striped culottes, waiting for the right moment to make my move. I was a lone wolf at recess, watching Ray kick the soccer ball, imagining the smile that would bloom across his face as soon as he read my irresistible confession. Finally the teachers called us in, and everyone was heading back into school, so I knew it was now or never. Or else I'd have to wait twenty-four hours until the next recess, which seemed unbearable. And so I walked up to Ray, shoved the index card in his face, and stared, silently, in his general direction.

He looked so cute as he read my manifesto. His hair had fallen over his eyes, so I couldn't read his expression, but I was sure it was one of sheer joy. Someday, hopefully starting today, Ray Espinoza and I would hold hands and pass notes to each other between classes. We would do whatever couples did—go on walks, share space, push each other into a swimming pool when we were feeling flirty. Then, just when I couldn't tolerate the uncertainty any longer, Ray folded the card in half, handed it back to me, and said, "I like Leslie P. I think she's my girlfriend." And then he headed back inside.

I stood and watched Ray and his tube socks walking away. How could this be happening? This is not how things went down in my imagination. I wrote a beautiful poem, had the courage to hand it over, and this guy wouldn't love me back. He loved Leslie P. This was all wrong. My culottes may have had sparkly gold stripes on them, but they weren't *that* bad. Were they? Recess was bullshit. Life was pain. And love could kiss my ten-year-old, culotte-covered ass.

After school I went home and told my mom what had happened. She was sweet and comforting at first, telling me that Ray was a fool and that I'd meet someone wonderful one day, when I had a little more life experience and had graduated from college. But when I wouldn't let Ray's betrayal go, and when I started walking around the house pinpointing all of Leslie's flaws ("she has a pet duck and it swims in their pool!" and "she's too tall for fifth grade!"), my mom sat me down, looked into my eyes, and laid it on me:

"Honey, there will always be someone richer, taller, smarter, and better looking than you. Do you understand what I mean? I love you, but you need to move on now."

It might sound harsh, but now that I'm older, I realize this is a mantra everyone should adopt. It's not meant to make you feel short or poor or homely or like your brain is pea-sized. Just the opposite: it's empowering, and if you have the right attitude, it'll help you realize that you need to be happy with where you are and stop making yourself miserable because you're not a six-foot-tall model with fabulous hair, immense wealth, and a hot husband named Ray Espinoza. It doesn't mean you can't reach your ultimate life dream—it just means you need to enjoy the attempt and be smart about how you get there. Or, how about *mostly smart*. We're not robots. We make mistakes. Just try to make wise decisions at least 72 percent of the time in your twenties, 87 percent of the time in your thirties, and 93.4 percent of the time from your forties until you reach the end of the line; do that, and you should be in pretty good shape.

Growing up, whenever my mom would throw that tough-love slogan my way, I would think (in an inner voice that was eerily similar to a female Napoleon Dynamite): "Geez, *thanks* Mom." It was only years later, when the hormones settled and real life came pounding at my door, that I finally got it. There will always be someone taller, smarter, and richer—and that's OK. If the cute soccer player doesn't love you back, if some bozo who bakes brownies for the boss got the promotion instead of you, or if your bank account isn't as impressive as Warren Buffett's, you can cry and blame the universe for your situation, you can suck it up and work to try and change it, or you can accept where you're at and move on. Life's too short to mope around over strappy gold Louboutins. If strappy gold Louboutins are what you want, then go ahead and make that happen, but just be smart about it, and make sure you're happy without them too. And don't come crying to me when a crazed, fashion-conscious criminal comes along, knocks you out with a frying pan, and steals them off your feet, leaving you alone, barefoot, and bling-less. I might shed one crocodile tear for you and your gold shoes, but that's it.

It's always extremely annoying when you grow up and realize that your parents were right, but they usually are. Unless your mom's mantra is: "Don't worry about finances; blow all your money, and when you do go into debt it'll be OK because you can sue someone or get a sugar daddy." No disrespect, but that's a mother who is:

C. Psychotic

On that note, before we move on to the next step in our quest to master the art of Brokenomics, let's examine one more scenario.

Again, unless your bank account was emptied by the world's

stealthiest identity thieves, the person/place/thing responsible for your finances is:

A. The universe

B. Your parents

C. Your next-door-neighbor Barbara

D. Leslie P. Espinoza

E. You

I trust you picked the correct answer, so congratulations! You've passed Brokenomics 101. You chose E right? If you picked A–D, let's just take a deep breath and continue. There is no judgment here. OK, maybe a little judgment, because E is the right answer. Whatever. Let's move on.

2

LAUGH IT UP

live in Los Angeles, a city that people love to hate. Usually their disdain comes from the fact that they believe the entire population of L.A. is made up of shallow, materialistic, annoying, flakey, narcissistic, money-hungry celebrities and wannabe celebrities. That's just not true. Maybe 68 percent of the city is that way, but the other 32 percent is made up of normal, down-to-earth, sane people who have no desire to act, write, direct, produce, or star in anything, except maybe a FaceTime video with their great-aunt Edith who is at death's door and in need of a little cheering up.

Living in a city like Los Angeles does grant you a front-row seat to the eccentricities and weird-ass habits of the super-rich, no matter what your bank statement reads. You might find yourself fashioning a voodoo doll out of your student loan bill one minute, and then wandering through a fancy house party with a bunch of actors and models and tubby bald men flanked by hot babes with fake boobs the next. These things happen. Examining the lifestyles of the rich and famous(ish) head-on has taught me a very important lesson when it comes to facing your financial situation, and that lesson is: you better have a freaking sense of humor.

As soon as possible, you need to learn to laugh it up. This is an ancient, fundamental law of the universe and a core tenet of

Brokenomics. It will serve you well when dealing with finances, internships, jobs, relationships, and life as you know it. Obviously you shouldn't start cracking jokes every time you bounce a check, but knowing how to take things in stride is essential. Let me elaborate.

You know that saying about poor people being crazy and rich people being eccentric? Don't believe it. If you saw Big Edie and Little Edie from *Grey Gardens* walking down the street wearing couture turbans and eating cat food out of a tin, what word would pop into your head: "crazy" or "eccentric"? OK, probably both. We all love Lady Gaga, but the woman got rich and then bought a ghost-detecting machine. At least, that's what the tabloids said. Whether she did or not, it's important to realize that it is OK that you're not a multimillionaire because, like the late, great Biggie Smalls warned us: more money sometimes means more problems. Mental problems.

Here's one trick I've learned that might help when you feel yourself coveting someone's car or purse or mansion: just imagine that the person is clinically insane. This is the same concept as when people tell you to imagine an audience in their underwear when you're nervous about public speaking. It lightens the mood and keeps you from getting sucked into a downward spiral of jealousy and self-doubt and emptiness. Someone else's pretty purse or souped-up car should never make you feel empty inside.

To prove this theory, let's examine Exhibit A: the case of the well-to-do taxidermist. A few years back I found myself wandering around a gorgeous, Japanese-style house owned by a thirty-year-old millionaire. It was a friend-of-a-friend scenario. On the island in the center of the kitchen, where most people would place a nice cheese tray or some spinach dip, there was a naked actress/model covered in sushi. I know Samantha did this for Smith Jerrod in *Sex and the City*, but it's not quite so cute in person, and it's definitely not appetizing. I asked the actress/model how long she got paid to lie there and whether she wanted a drink. She was very cool. I have a ton of respect for actors because they have to do things like pose as human hors d'oeuvres on their path to fame and fortune. That's a tough gig.

Back to Exhibit A. Eventually I wound up talking to the girlfriend of this millionaire host. She had a beautiful, unique purse, the kind you can't find at Marshalls or Zara, and I admit it made me a little jealous. She told me she was a jewelry designer and shoved a necklace with a tiny bird-head charm toward my face before I could defend myself. This was no Neiman Marcus–worthy silver or gold bird head. This thing was real. As in: once alive, frolicking in the treetops and regurgitating worms into its baby's beak.

"Oh. That's . . . is it real?" I asked, terrified I'd just been given some horrible disease. Between this and the sushi display, it was becoming a pretty unpleasant party. "Yep! I find dead birds on the beach and taxidermy the heads at home. Aren't they cute?" Just picture this bird necklace—do you think "cute" is the best way to describe it? I have nothing against taxidermy or jewelry designers, but come on. I had to laugh (inside, secretly, to myself). She told me she'd make me one of her bird-head necklaces, and, being a Southerner and thus prone to putting on a happy face and lying through my teeth in the most awkward of situations, I said, "I'd love that!" Then we parted ways, and suddenly her beautiful purse didn't have such a hold on me anymore. Instead, I just laughed it off, decided that she was insane, blocked the little bird head out of my mind, and went to fill up on free champagne.

Now let's look at Exhibit B, the closing argument in my Laugh It Up thesis. A few months after my run-in with the taxidermist, I found myself at a "truffle party in the hills" thrown by a photographer I'd met at the bird-head party. It was in the Hollywood Hills, and she made homemade chocolate truffles—hence the name. All of her photos were displayed around the house, which meant that everywhere you looked there were black-and-white shots of naked women on European rooftops. I was alone and adrift in a roomful of boobs.

After browsing the photos for a few minutes, I sat on the couch with my truffle and decided to strike up a conversation with a woman who was decked out in a floor-length, glittery pink 1960s ball gown.

If Yoko Ono and a *Cosmo* model were thrown into a test tube and stirred around, this woman would pop out of the smoke. Her dress was a little bonkers (especially since everyone else at the party wore jeans and brought their dogs), but she was also wearing the most gorgeous bracelet I'd ever laid eyes on—it had gemstones I'd never seen and looked like it was once owned by Marie Antoinette. I was jealous. It was so unfair. I wasn't even wearing a bracelet.

I decided to investigate.

"So, what do you do?" I asked. Where I'm from, this is a perfectly normal question. Maybe I should have cut to the chase and commented on the bracelet first, but she was a little intimidating.

"What do I do?"

"Yeah," I replied. "You know, for work or for fun or . . . anything."

She paused beneath her mane of black locks. I braced myself. Dramatic pauses are always so exciting.

"My life is very vivid," she whisper-growled before turning away from me entirely. How rude! Plus, "My life is very vivid"? Is that a job? Or even a hobby? Does she sprinkle peyote into her morning oatmeal? Maybe she was a deep-sea diver, or an astronaut—the two most vivid jobs I can think of. I never got to find out what she meant since she was so snooty/crazy/tweaked on LSD, but whatever a "vivid life" is, I'm pretty sure you don't have to be loaded to live one. And just like that, the Marie Antoinette bracelet didn't seem as badass once I realized that it was wrapped around the wrist of a maniac.

So you see, when you're feeling less than fancy and coveting someone's bling, you need to laugh it off. And remember to imagine that the other person is completely insane, which she very well might be.

> **Note.** "Laugh It Off" is a healthy coping strategy for when you're feeling crappy about your financial situation and someone with a gorgeous purse, house, or bracelet makes you feel like a hobo. It's not saying that all multimillionaires are insane. Only some. Maybe 63 percent.

3

BE YOUR OWN LIFE COACH

I t seems to me that one day we all woke up and life coaches had suddenly become a thing. Throughout history we've had oracles and seers and therapists and Oprah, but somewhere along the way in the not-so-distant past, professional life coaches busted onto the scene to help us get organized, reach our goals, and uncover our hidden potential.

That's all wonderful, but hiring a life coach can be a pricey ordeal. In 2011, *Harvard Business Review* reported that life coaching was a one-billion-a-year racket, ahem, I mean, industry. Evidently, a lot of us really need help getting our shit together. Sometimes life coaches will give you a free intro session, but beyond that you better get ready to pay them cash money. Or you could write a check or use PayPal or promise them your first-born child—your choice. If they're new age-y, you might be able to pay them with a "love donation," which, factoring in ethereal tolls like karma, shame, and guilt, equals roughly $5 to $60 dollars a session, depending on your moral compass.

Before you run out and start handing over your hard-earned wages to someone who uses words like "quantum healing" and "multi-dimensional third-eye meditation," I suggest you first try and become your own life coach. Obviously you are not an unbiased outside party, but here are five tips that might help you save some cash and become your own guru:

Get Off the Couch. If you're slouching around your apartment day in and day out, complaining that nothing is happening for you and it's so annoying that you're not successful and rich and all-powerful, you need to get the hell off your ass, metaphorically speaking. Literally getting up from the couch is a good idea too. This also applies to barstools, beds, linoleum floors, ditches, and beanbags. There is nothing worse than a person who is all talk and no action. Ophelia drowned herself in a brook because Hamlet couldn't get off his ass and get out of his own head. Don't be a Hamlet. Get up.

Master the Tao of the To-Do List. This sounds simple, and it is. It's also extremely effective. I write a to-do list several times a week. (I usually have to rewrite them because I have a very serious doodling addiction and after a few hours I can't read what I've written, but that's another story.) To set goals, it helps to write them down, so think of it as a treasure map to your future awesomeness. Mark up a white board, type into your phone, or go old school and scribble on a notepad— doodles optional. The act of writing down both what you want to accomplish and the steps you'll need to get there will help you reach your goal, inch by agonizing-yet-fulfilling little inch.

Treat Yourself. Even though you shouldn't buy yourself a mink stole every time you mark something off your to-do list, it's important to reward yourself when you reach milestones. If you've spent the last six weeks sending out résumés and you finally got an interview, go reward yourself with a nice but reasonable dinner, a concert, or a new hairdo. If you finally got the guts to ask for that raise, go get those shoes you've been eyeballing. It'll help make all the other steps in your journey much more tolerable. Just make sure the shoes are an affordable splurge, rather than an "I have to declare bankruptcy" splurge.

Never Assume. This bit of wisdom was burned into my brain by a grad school professor, and now whenever I start to utter the phrase, "Oh, I just assumed . . ." I'm overcome with guilt and shame, and I come pretty close to flogging myself. The world owes you nothing, so the sooner you stop assuming things will happen in a certain way the better off you'll be. I don't mean you should become a nihilist, but when you stop expecting things to turn out a certain way, and stop assuming, you'll find your QUANTUM HAPPY PLACE. Just kidding. But you will be a much happier, more productive person. You'll be pleasantly surprised more often than you'll be morbidly disappointed. It's OK that the world owes you nothing. That just means it's your job to go out and make things happen.

The 24-Hour Pity Party. In life, you will face hardship, rejection, and setbacks. You want to have a five-bedroom house, a CEO position, an Audi, and two kids by the time you're thirty? That may or may not happen. I hope it does. But a lot of the fun and adventure of life comes from the struggle to get to where you're going, financially or otherwise. I know that sounds like life-coach BS, but it's true. In order to deal with the ups and downs (mainly the downs), you need to learn to allow yourself a finite time to stew. If a goal isn't reached by the "perfect" time, or if you face a setback, rather than mope around for a week or two or ten cursing the universe and driving your friends and family to drink every time your name pops up on caller ID (à la Hamlet), give yourself twenty-four to forty-eight hours (or even five hours if you're really into tough love) to be pissed off and wallow in your misery. You can actually train yourself to master this technique. Start practicing now, and soon enough you'll be pretty shocked at how quickly you start bouncing back and forging ahead. If you do this often enough, you almost become a machine (in a good way), and with every setback you're less likely to wind up curled in the fetal position spooning a half-eaten pizza and a bottle of tequila like a movie montage cliché.

So, if you're tempted to get a life coach but that's not in your budget, these five steps will save you money as you figure out your goals and start to move toward them. You can also pray silently, chant your wishes to a clock every time it strikes/shows/beams 11:11, or become a Wiccan and cast some cool spells. I happen to believe that the five steps listed above are a little more effective. I've never practiced witchcraft (except for that brief time in seventh grade), but I am a sucker for the 11:11 chant. You're praying to a clock that may or may not be 100 percent accurate. That's called hope.

4

STOP TRYING TO KEEP UP WITH THE JONESES (OR THE CARTERS OR THE KARDASHIANS)

I t starts when you're in diapers. You see someone holding a bright, shiny object and you must have it in your hands that instant. In middle school, the new cheerleader has a designer backpack, so you want one too. You lust after the gorgeous gowns celebs wear on the red carpet, you drool over the Swarovski baby bathtub that Blue Ivy Carter had, you see everyone at work wearing Marc Jacobs suits and you feel pressured to get one too. It's exhausting, and never-ending. Stop it. Stop it so you can hold onto your sanity and keep your finances in check.

Sometimes that's easier said than done. Who doesn't want beautiful clothes, a great home, and fabulous bath products from France? Sign me up. The problem is that this phenomenon known as "keeping up with the Joneses" is no longer just about envying your neighbor's awesome butter churn or badass weathervane. Thanks to tabloid news, the Internet, and social media, we can peer into the fifteen-bedroom homes of celebs or see a $16,000 bar tab on Rich Kids of Instagram.

I'm all for retail therapy when you really need it, because sometimes buying the sexiest miniskirt you can find or blowing some cash at Hooters on a pitcher and some wings (that's what they're known for—the wings) right after a breakup is actually good for you, since your mental state after a breakup is usually a little psycho. It's wise to do whatever it takes to pull yourself out of that funk, as long as you're not hurting anyone or doing any irreparable damage to your reputation. But overspending so that you can have the latest, trendiest things in life and follow what everyone else is doing will get you into a financial pickle faster than you can say "Kate Middleton."

> **Overspending so that you can have the latest, trendiest things in life and follow what everyone else is doing will get you into a financial pickle faster than you can say "Kate Middleton."**

If you actually follow through and buy the things you're lusting after even if you can't afford them, you'll eventually find yourself pawning your Louis Vuitton luggage for cash or, even worse, sleeping in your Louis Vuitton luggage under a bridge because you can't afford rent—but you keep clinging to your fancy valise because it makes you feel human and reminds you of the good old days. But do you really need to go into debt for a $39,000 alligator backpack just because your coworker has one? Even if you can afford it, paying $39,000 for a backpack is pretty ludicrous. It's a freaking backpack.

Plus, you never know what someone else's money situation is. In person, you might be seeing a superstar with a Bentley and a bling-y backpack, but on paper, you could see their name on top of several bills from creditors marked: FINAL NOTICE. It happens more often than you imagine.

And check this out: a 2011 Fidelity Investments survey found that four out of ten American millionaires said they "didn't feel rich." In order to feel rich they said they'd need to have an average of $7.5 million. That might mean that when they reach the $7.5 million mark and their new neighbor is a billionaire, they'll still feel unsatisfied. One thing that people in every single tax bracket share is the capacity for some serious money envy. Some of us are jealous of a coworker's shiny 2015 Camry, and others are seething because they don't have a 2016 customized Bentley like the mogul next door. The objects might be different, but the feeling is the same.

Think of it this way: You know those couples that are so wildly, passionately in love that every time they gaze into each other's eyes you suddenly feel like puking? Where every day is a ticker tape parade celebrating the fact that they're cosmic soul mates, and each time their hands touch, a tectonic plate shifts and a shooting star flies over a unicorn's head? Those are the couples that usually end up in a *The War of the Roses*–style breakup where they want to poke each other's eyeballs out with a priceless heirloom or smash over the other's head the Ming dynasty vase they bought at auction. On the outside, their relationship looks blissful. Behind closed doors, it's *WrestleMania*, only with very pricey props and real violence.

It can be the same with the people who run around flaunting the fact that their life is so fabulous—in turn making you jealous of their Balenciaga handbag and their Prada sable coat. Inside the pocket of that coat, you might find a wad of audit notices and unpaid parking tickets. And, just like imagining that wildly wealthy people are clinically insane so you can laugh it up and feel better about your life, when you find yourself trying to keep up with Mr. Jones you can close your eyes and imagine those audit notices and past-due bills tucked into his sable coat or buried underneath the rose bush in his English garden. While it's not entirely friendly to wish all that debt upon them, it is a healthy way to keep yourself in check.

It's important to think about your finances as a long-term thing, rather than as a day-to-day, carpe diem, I-want-to-die-before-age-thirty-like-James-Dean-so-I-may-as-well-splurge-on-this-watch-I-can't-afford thing. Now, I know it's hard to imagine saving money early on if you're not making much or if you're eighteen years old and you think retirement is something that happens to old wrinkly people. But guess what—one day, hopefully, you will be one of those old wrinkly people, and you won't be dead yet, and you'll be really sorry that you have zero money saved because you blew it all on monogrammed wooden and leather beach racquets. Do you really want to be struggling and hustling when you're in your seventies?

For many of us, setting aside money each month might seem impossible, but it'd be smart to put even 5 or 10 percent of your salary into a savings account every month as soon as you can, ideally working your way up to 20 percent. You don't have to hoard your salary and forgo all fun just so you have some retirement money, but if you're spending carelessly because you feel pressured to have what a neighbor or a coworker or a mortal enemy owns, it's time to stop keeping up with the Joneses. Who the hell cares what they think anyway?

The correct answer is: "Not me!"

If the little voice in your head answered, "Uh . . . me?" then you need to work on mastering the "visualize past-due notices in Mr. Jones's sable coat pocket" technique and get your priorities in line. When it comes to finances, if you care what other people think, you're screwed. You're strong, and you have an endless reserve of willpower. OK, even if it's not an *endless* reserve, I'm betting it's at least a little trickle of willpower. Even that should help you resist the temptation to blow your salary on things you can't afford. Besides, if you wake up in thirty years and realize you've saved a decent chunk of money, you'll probably feel like you've won the lottery, which will make the "sacrifice" all the more empowering.

II.

THE BASICS

Don't think money does everything or you are
going to end up doing everything for money.
—Voltaire

I had the most absurd nightmare. I was poor and no one liked me.
—Louis Winthorpe III, *Trading Places*

5

NOBODY LIKES A KLEPTO

klep·to·ma·nia [KLEP-tuh-mey-nee-uh], *noun*: a persistent neurotic impulse to steal especially without economic motive.[1]

Once upon a time, I was a klepto. I didn't do anything drastic like stuff Nordstrom prom dresses into my backpack. The "cool" girls in my high school did, but I was way too wimpy. I wanted to get the hell out of my hometown, which already felt like a jail cell to me—I didn't need an actual jail cell to rub in that fact. But my kleptomania did stem from a neurotic impulse, which I like to call my "Post College Existential Meltdown," or PCEM if you want to get scientific about it.

The first year after college can be rough. You're tossed out into the "real world" with a résumé and some T.J. Maxx interview outfits. Mere months earlier, lying in a grassy sculpture garden and reading Henry James for your three-o'clock lit class was considered responsible. You weren't just discussing feminist discourse in *The Portrait of a Lady*, you were working your way toward a bright future and a job. But in the wake of graduation, reading in a garden on a Wednesday afternoon is considered lazy, ridiculous, and a big fat

---

1. By permission. From Merriam-Webster's Collegiate® Dictionary, 11th Edition ©2014 by Merriam-Webster, Inc. (www.Merriam-Webster.com)

waste of time. Youth is definitely wasted on the young, and there's nothing like a post-college panic attack to help you realize that.

After college, I temped for a few months until I got a job at an entertainment industry agency, which paid $18,000 a year. My roommate, a very smart psychology major, worked at KB Toys in the mall selling Barbie Dream Houses and Buzz Lightyear action figures. When we weren't earning our millions (of pennies), we sat on our stoop, drank a lot of boxed wine, and talked about the good old days of college as if we were eighty-year-olds reminiscing about our youth.

What does this have to do with my kleptomania story, you might ask. Well, we got in the habit of taking toilet paper from work because my roommate and I were too cheap to buy it.[2] How embarrassing is that? It's not like t.p. is that pricey. We couldn't afford a trip to Abu Dhabi, but we could definitely afford some Charmin. I also took pens, paper, rubber bands, and staplers from work, just in case we needed to write a note or staple something together. So, while our kleptomania wasn't due to economic *need* exactly, it was due to emotional stress caused by our economic *situation*. And by our maturity level. And by the fact that our bosses were dickheads.

Look, since Oliver Twist truly needed that gruel, I wouldn't tell if he stole an extra helping. I'd cheer him on. But if you're feeling the need to steal stuff because you're experiencing your own PCEM, or even just for the thrill of it, I wouldn't advocate thievery unless you're a modern-day Clyde Barrow or Bonnie Parker. To help you decide whether the criminal route is for you, take a look at some of the pros and cons I've put together about becoming a klepto:

Pros
- Free stuff
- A fleeting adrenaline rush . . .

Cons
- . . . that quickly morphs into paranoia and panic and possible jail time

---

2. Note that we prioritized boxed wine over essential toiletries.

- Bail bonds

- Handcuffs

- Public humiliation

- It looks terrible on your résumé

- Karma

- Nobody likes a klepto

So, if your boss treats you like crap, and stealing some two-ply makes you feel better about the situation, then go ahead. Otherwise, let these "pros" and "cons" be your guide. There's enough financial pressure in life. Adding bail bonds to the list just seems irresponsible.

6

THE JOY OF HAGGLING

H aggling gets a bad rap. It shouldn't just be reserved for the times you're crossing back into California from Tijuana, still drunk from the Buttery Nipple shots you had the night before, trying to sweeten the price on that Elvis blanket you think you need. I haggle all the time—within reason. It's not about being cheap; it's about being frugal. There's a difference. Keep in mind that whenever you're haggling you need to be nice and calm and polite. No bullying, yelling, or threatening to call the authorities.

Here's a rundown of the good, the bad, and the ugly when it comes to haggling:

THE GOOD

Electronics/Computers. First, you should always get a warranty. But say it expired, or say it's too late and you didn't get the warranty and there you are at the Genius Bar. Here's a trick I learned when I was laid-off and unemployed and I woke up one day to find that my laptop would suddenly only work if the screen was set at a forty-five-degree angle (I still feel a phantom pain in my neck whenever I think about it). When I finally went to the Genius Bar and was told it would cost $250 just to have someone look at my sad little laptop, I remained calm while I pled my case, and the very sweet, double-helix-tattooed employee leaned in conspiratorially and told me to call the 1-800 number and "use trigger words." I asked what a "trigger word" was and he said, "'Inconvenience.' Use that a lot; it makes them feel guilty. And 'corporate responsibility.' That scares them." And you know what? It worked. You can also tell them you're a "loyal customer," and say, "please." You might want to spend some time practicing your pitiful, "Thank you, sir, may I have another?" face in the mirror before going in for the kill. It can't hurt.

Cable/Internet. There is no shame in haggling with behemoths like Time Warner Cable or Verizon. These aren't mom-and-pop operations we're talking about. If cable is an expense you feel is worth it, but the monthly rate mysteriously goes up (it happens—a lot) or you just want to see if you can get maybe $20 off your monthly bill, first cut to the chase and ask for a manager. If that doesn't work, threaten to leave them for another provider and then sit back and listen to them type who knows what into their computer, crunch some numbers, and get your bill down. If your request is within reason, they'll usually make it happen. The phone reps are humans with beating hearts, not corporate drones. If you do get a corporate drone, call back repeatedly until you get a real person. This may require patience and time, so clear your schedule.

Cars. You should always haggle with a car salesperson. It might not be fun, but it's a must. Also, never, ever act impressed with anything they show you. Apathy is key here. Heated steering wheel? Who cares. Massage chairs and genuine leather from Italy? Whatever. Sculpted side mirrors? Lame. If you act excited about the bells and whistles, they're less likely to get desperate and lower the price. Instead, act as if you've had heated steering wheels and rear-seat DVD players since birth. It'll throw them off their game. You should also ask them to cover the cost of any registration and DMV fees, and try to get them to throw in the first month's payment as well (as long as you're putting money down). If they balk, in a very firm tone reply, "Well, I don't want to have to walk out of here, but . . ." That'll terrify them. They definitely don't want you to walk off; they want you to drive off—in the car they've just sold you. And if you're really freaking out, remember this: when buying a car, don't listen to your heart; listen to the panic attack symptoms erupting all over your body. Then walk away and take a nap if you're not ready. You're buying a car, not a candy bar. Don't sign the papers if your hands are shaking uncontrollably and you feel like puking in a nearby trashcan. And if they're saying that the deal they're offering will only last until midnight—they're bluffing. Go home and think it over.

Late Fees. As long as you're not constantly late, you can usually get a late fee reversed, whether you're asking your credit card company, your bank, or your cable company. Just tell them it's a one-time thing, you'll never do it again, and thank them when they say, "OK, fine." Then try to pay all your bills on time. Setting up a recurring payment should do the trick—plus you won't have to deal with stamps or late fees.

Gym Memberships. Like car salespeople, gym managers are primed for a haggling session. See if they'll knock off a portion of the registration cost or lower the monthly rate. If they're being tough, tell them you're going to march, jog, do plyometric hops, or sprint over to a rival gym. That should do the trick.

Furniture. If you're buying furniture at Macy's or Target, you're definitely not going to get the price down unless it's damaged or you're dealing with a rogue salesperson who wants to stick it to The Man. But if it's a privately owned shop, they'll usually work with you, unless you're being ridiculous. Don't ask to pay $100 for a $4,000 couch. If you do that, I say they're allowed to charge you $4,100 for the couch.

Bicycles. It's perfectly acceptable to try and knock the price down when you're buying a $400 bicycle. I don't know how a Harley salesperson would feel if you tried to haggle, but if it's a mountain bike or a Beach Cruiser or a unicycle, it's worth a conversation. Especially if it's a unicycle—it's just one wheel! I'm not sure if that tactic will work, since I've never bought a unicycle, but you can try.

Mortgage Rates. Shop around, get quotes, make sure your credit score is stellar, and you should be able to talk about lowering things like processing fees. You can also keep renting so you won't have to deal with all this crap. It's your choice.

Other things worth a good haggle: salary, hotel rooms, garage sales (obvi), medical bills (you can at least get a payment plan), rental cars, eyeglasses, farmers' market produce, art, and wedding costs. Good luck with that last one though—the wedding industry exists to tempt you and suck your bank account dry, so you'll need superhuman haggling skills in this arena. Stay strong.

THE BAD

Restaurant bills (unless there was an insect in your food or the server slapped you across the face for no reason), school tuition (not happening), movie tickets (also not happening), ice cream cones, lemonade stand refills, Girl Scout cookies, a Slurpee, a game of blackjack, your taxes, a ticket to a charity event, a free lunch, a tattoo. I mean, they're etching permanent ink into your skin with a needle—do not piss them off.

AND THE UGLY

If you've offered to treat a friend, relative, lover, coworker, or any other human being on the planet to drinks or dinner or a piece of Key lime pie, never, ever haggle over the price in front of them—unless they're your lifelong nemesis and you're avenging a murder in an extremely wimpy way. Even then . . . probably not a good idea.

7

ALWAYS TIP,
OR YOU'RE GOING TO HELL

I f you can afford to valet your car and/or get it washed, go out to eat, hang out at a bar or club where someone is standing in the bathroom handing out paper towels, or pay for a six-dollar Spanish latte made by someone who is forced to wear a vest and steam milk all day, you can afford to tip. It doesn't have to be extravagant, but it better be something.

Or you're going to hell.

8

HOW TO STEP AWAY
FROM THE LOTTO TICKETS

We all love seeing lottery winners dance around on the news and cry and talk about the house they're going to buy as they clutch a big cardboard check for $250 million. It's the American dream. It symbolizes hope and optimism. If they've struggled all their life, it's the ultimate financial fairy tale. Even so, the temptation to blow your paycheck on lotto tickets is a dangerous one, and if that's what you've been doing, it's time for an intervention. It'll be fun.

We've all had those days where you wake up and just get *that feeling*. Occasionally, for no apparent reason, everyone feels lucky—like, if something good is going to happen, it's going to happen on that very day. On days like that, skipping over to the corner bodega to buy some lotto tickets seems totally logical. The stars are aligned and the breeze is just right and the universe is conspiring to make you a Powerball winner. It's a totally rational feeling.

Still, there's a reason lotto tickets cost just one dollar: so people buy armloads of them and then assuage their guilt by saying, "They only cost a dollar!" It's the same with gambling. I love betting a buck here and there at the horse track, and I'm no stranger to fifty-cent roulette tables, but buying oodles of lotto tickets each week in your quest to "get rich quick" is not a savvy move. Plus, it's not nearly as fun as sitting around a table, betting on double zero, and watching a wheel spin around. I don't care how much money you have—if you're buying lotto tickets in excess, you need to step away from the Scratchers.

If you're secretly clutching your weekly bundle of Pick 3 slips right now, let's look at what happened to a friend of mine whose lotto mania got so out of hand her husband actually did have to stage an intervention. Let's call her Sarah, and let's dub him James. I'll use my initials, to add a touch of mystery.

DG: *How did your lotto addiction start?*

Sarah: *I started buying lotto tickets because I felt lucky one day. I really had it in my head that if I played enough, we would hit it big.*

DG: *What did you imagine you'd do if you won?*

Sarah: *I kept thinking that if I won, I would put college money away for both kids, give some to my family, and buy a house. Then I'd put the rest away for my kids when they got older.*

DG: *Did you ever win?*

Sarah: *Once I won almost $200 and instead of keeping it, I used it all on lotto tickets then only won $50 back. I was so mad at myself I didn't even tell James. As far as spending the money on lotto tickets, I usually didn't even think about it. I did get really upset if I lost but I would say to myself I could win on the next one.*

DG: *When did the intervention happen?*

Sarah: *I had a true lotto addiction. James had the intervention with me one night, and he told me that lotto tickets weren't the answer to getting money or becoming rich. I said, "Well if we don't play, we can't win." He said I had a crazy look in my eyes and that he was worried.*

DG: *Well you didn't get divorced, so how did you resolve it?*

Sarah: *He said I had to wait three weeks to buy a $5 ticket and that I could only play with winnings. If I lost, then I couldn't buy a* *lotto ticket for another three weeks. He gave me an allowance to buy lotto tickets once a month.*

DG: *Are you a reformed woman, as far as lotto ticket go?*

Sarah: *I'm not obsessed anymore, but I did buy one the other day and won two bucks, and then I bought a $2 one and lost. I didn't buy another one.*

DG: *What advice would you give to people who are buying lotto tickets every week?*

Sarah: *I would say it's OK to play sometimes, because if you don't play you won't win.*

I'm not sure how helpful James's intervention was. Sarah did cut back on her lotto spending though, and I haven't seen her hoarding Scratchers with that look in her eyes, so she's definitely on the mend. Unless you want to force your husband or wife or best friend to stage an intervention, take Sarah's experience as a word of warning. If you absolutely want to play the lotto, do it in moderation. Extreme moderation. If one ticket a week doesn't put a dent in your savings or put your finances in any jeopardy whatsoever, go for it and may The Force be with you. I hope to see you dancing around on CNN with $200 million coming your way.

> **How's this for an alternative to spending money on lotto tickets: set it up so that $25 magically moves from your checking to your savings account each month, starting now, in perpetuity.**

Quick reality check though. How's this for an alternative to spending money on lotto tickets: set it up so that $25 magically moves from your checking to your savings account each month, starting now, in perpetuity. Do it if you're eighteen; do it if you're thirty-eight. Imagine if you're saving twenty-five bucks every month for five, ten, fifteen years. Instead of spending $3,000 on lotto tickets over ten years, you'll have $3,000 in the bank. It might not be a $1 million Powerball win, but it's something. But if, every once in a while, when the breeze is just right and the universe and stars are all aligned and you *just have that feeling*, go to the corner store, pick up *one* lotto ticket, and see what happens. As the late, great film director Robert Altman said, "To play it safe is not to play." He was talking about movies and creativity and not Mega Millions, but still. If it's not breaking the bank, it's worth taking a $1 chance every once in a while.

But if your eyes start to bug out every time you see a Scratcher, you have a problem, and you need to go back to the beginning of this chapter and memorize every single word. Or at least memorize this: step away from the lotto tickets. Then imagine yourself alone, destitute, and using a pile of worthless Powerball receipts as a blanket. That should do the trick.

9

WHY HAVE A BABY WHEN YOU CAN JUST GET A NICE POTTED PLANT?

efore you're all, "Oh my god I love babies she's so cold-hearted her womb must be a ball of dust and cobwebs!" let me just state for the record that I adore infants, tiny children, and humanity at large. As long as the kid doesn't share any personality traits with Damien from *The Omen* or Veruca "Daddy I want an Oompa Loompa!" Salt from *Willy Wonka*, I think they're pretty fantastic. Babies can spit up on me all they want—they're innocent, adorable little people, and they can't help it. I really mean that. I'm not volunteering to be a one-woman spit-up receptacle or anything; I just really need you to know that I love babies.

As they say, no one is ever ready to have a baby. You can't perfectly plan for it and wait until you have $5 million set aside—you just have to go for it, if it's what you really want. Babies cost money, and they'll still cost money when they're six, eleven, sixteen, and, these days, twenty-four. I don't yet have a human money pit—a.k.a. a baby of my own—but I do have nieces and nephews and lots of FWBs (Friends With Babies, not Benefits), so I have a unique perspective when it comes to the financial implications of having kids. The wisdom I'm about to impart has never been uttered before, so brace yourselves: having children is expensive. I know—it's pretty revolutionary. I'll let you sit with that a minute.

An August 2014 report from the U.S. Department of Agriculture revealed that, for a middle-income family, a child adds between $12,800 and $14,970 in yearly expenses.[3] Let's contrast that with the cost of a nice little potted plant, which will set you back about fifteen bucks, give or take a few dollars. Plants bring you joy, life (oxygen and whatnot), and lots of laughs. OK, maybe they won't bring you lots of laughs unless you're living a vivid, peyote-laced life, but

The wisdom I'm about to impart has never been uttered before, so brace yourselves: having children is expensive.

they're nice enough. They don't talk back, they don't tell you they hate you six times a day from the ages of twelve to fourteen, and they don't require college tuition. To also play devil's advocate: plants don't have limbs full of cute Michelin Man fat rolls, their smiles don't have the power to obliterate all the darkness in the universe, and they'd look pretty weird in a monogrammed onesie. So it's a toss-up.

I'm not saying money should stop you from bringing a child into this world. There are financially savvy parents out there. And then there are parents who throw their children $10,000 birthday parties with ponies, $500 tiered cakes, flowers flown in from Africa, and ice castles. So there's some wiggle room when it comes to the yearly cost of rearing a child.

It's a personal decision whether you have kids or not. As you're making that decision, keep in mind that there are some ill-advised reasons to have an adorable but costly little baby, such as:

- Everyone else is doing it

---

3. Lino, Mark. (2014). Expenditures on Children by Families, 2013. U.S. Department of Agriculture, Center for Nutrition Policy and Promotion. Miscellaneous Publication No. 1528-2013.

- You're bored
- You want a fun doll to dress up
- You want to send its photo to *People* magazine so they'll publish it in their "Moms & Babies" section
- You want to run for political office and having a human of your own will help your campaign. Gross.

There's a lot of pressure to have kids. But badass women like Dolly Parton, Ellen DeGeneres, Margaret Cho, Helen Mirren, and Oprah Winfrey don't have kids, and you don't see them spontaneously combusting. This is just something to think about now that you're taking responsibility for your financial future.

If you've put a lot of thought into it, and if a potted plant or a puppy just isn't enough, to follow are some wise money tips from my very own crew of FWBs. While some of these friends are more cynical than others, they're all fabulous parents:

> *"Never buy the baby wipe warmer. Not worth the money. And seriously . . . what baby needs the wipe to be warm?"*

> *"When you're in the hospital, take home all the baby stuff they give you and ask for more. I emptied every drawer."*

> *"Refuse to pay for 'mommy groups'—that's bullshit."*

> *"Invite all your rich friends to the baby shower and send out 'welcome our new baby' announcements to see if you can score more presents."*

> *"I guess I saved money by not buying anything for myself for a few years."*

So there you have it. If you can afford to have four kids and monogram all their "John Johns," then more power to you. If not, remember you can pop over to Home Depot and buy a fern or a fiddle-leaf fig. They might not be as cute and precious and animated as a baby, but they're a hell of a lot cheaper.

10

WHY YOU SHOULD NEVER "JUST" USE YOUR CREDIT CARDS

R emember that life-changing pop quiz back in chapter 1? The one about the person who gets a job and blows all her money on designer shoes and a fancy dinner? Hopefully you'll recall this answer:

This behavior is:
B. Totally cool because you can put it all on your credit card

That answer was incorrect. If you did choose B, or if you mentally coaxed your pen away from B and circled D (Irresponsible as hell) just because you were too embarrassed to go with your true instinct, I understand your impulses. It's fun to have nice things. It's not fun to have nice things and then wake up one day to find that you're $10,000 in debt. That's why it's time to take a solemn vow. Take three deep breaths, stare into the closest mirrored surface, and chant: "There's no such thing as 'just' using a credit card," fourteen times while twirling in circles, and you're done.

It would be nice if it were that easy. Credit card debt is real, and no amount of chanting and twirling will make it disappear.

Before you start racking up a Visa bill the size of Bavaria's GDP, you should silently remind yourself, several times a day, that there's no such thing as "just" using your credit card. When you catch yourself saying, "It's so expensive, but . . . I'll just use my credit card," that's your signal to put the card back in your wallet and walk away from the thing you can't afford. If you try that tactic and you still find yourself handing over your Amex, you need to:

1. Leave the cards at home and use cash, so that when you pay for things you realize it's real, tangible funds you're handing off, and not some magical cash flow made of fairy dust and chocolate sprinkles.

2. When you feel ready to carry your credit cards again, test yourself: use your cards sparingly and pay them off, in full, every month. If you find that you can't do this, stop using them.

3. Start a support group. Make a pact with one or two of your friends to keep each other in check. Be completely honest with each other about what you're spending, how much you're paying off, and what your level of debt is. Honesty and shame are very good motivators, and they can work wonders for your will power.

Yes, using credit cards wisely and paying them off on time can help build your credit, and that's a very positive financial move, but it's not Monopoly money, and you will have to pay it back, with interest if you're late. It's not that you shouldn't use them—hell, a woman couldn't even get a credit card in her own name until Congress passed the Equal Credit Opportunity Act in 1974. Our grandmothers and great-grandmothers are probably proud as hell that we can get and use our own damn cards. So use them, but wisely. You can get frequent-flier miles and hotel discounts by using the right cards wisely, so just proceed with caution.

One caveat: if your idea of using them wisely is blowing $2,000 at Bloomingdale's even though you're already in debt, try this Brokenomics Advanced XTREME Method™[4]:

1. Place your credit card(s) on a flat surface
2. Take two deep breaths
3. Close your eyes and imagine yourself being buried alive by however many $1 bills equal your debt
4. Choose to live (there's nothing glamorous about suffocating to death under a mound of money—that shit is germy)
5. Grab some scissors
6. Cut your cards into a million pieces (two to five pieces will work too)
7. Do a celebration dance: jigging, Krumping, two-stepping, the Cat Daddy—your choice

When you're finished, make a plan and pledge not to get another credit card until your debt is paid.[5] If there's something you just *have* to have, do what your ancestors did and save up the cash until you can legitimately afford it. You *have* to have food, shelter, and water. You don't really have to have an Alexander McQueen clutch or a TAG Heuer Monaco 24 Limited Edition Men's Watch in Stainless Steel, awesome as they may be. You'll live without them, I swear.

---

4. Advanced XTREME Method isn't actually trademarked. You can steal it if you want to.
5. FYI: Fleeing to Bolivia and living off the grid does not count as paying your debt.

11

WEBMD IS NOT AN MD

Depending on the country you live in, health insurance is either a birthright or a huge, expensive, nightmarish pain in the ass. Have you ever heard anyone utter the words, "I just love the healthcare system"? (Not including CEOs of Blue Shield and Kaiser Permanente.) Did you hear about the homeless man who in 2013 tried to rob a bank for $1 so he could get free healthcare, care of the Department of Corrections? I think many of us can empathize with his mania and admire his bold action. It didn't work though. He reportedly got slapped with a $40,000 bail bill, so please don't follow his lead. Still, I salute his efforts.

Like many people around the world, in 2010, I was laid-off from my job, which means I had to crumple up all my Post-it notes (which had incredibly important information like SHEILA X3546), hand in my laptop, weather alternating surges of elation and despair, and, most important, say sayonara to my paycheck and my benefits. Those goodbyes were not easy.

Now, what I'm about to admit should be filed away in your DO NOT TRY THIS AT HOME memory file-folder thingy. I imagine everyone has metaphorical, multicolored file folders hanging in their hippocampus, but obviously I'm not a physician. Regard-less, my shameful admission, which I'm telling you because taking responsibility for your finances means admitting when you're a jackass, is: after my boss gave me the boot, I went two years without health insurance. Actually I did sign up for Blue Shield for two months, until I realized how much I was paying. Then I panicked and canceled it.

I would never, ever recommend going without health insurance. Now, as of 2014, everyone in the U.S. has a more fair chance of having coverage, but it wasn't affordable when I was laid-off, and I just couldn't fathom paying between $200 and $400 a month (at least) for coverage. Fortunately I was pretty healthy during that time, which allowed me to run around like an imbecile and not think about the consequences. Actually, I did think about the consequences, constantly. I just didn't want to pay that bill. My reasoning was so ridiculous that I'm just now realizing I may have had more in common with the $1 bank robber than I thought. It seems like some of our similarities included: irrational behavior, faulty logic, and a fiscal death wish.

One way that I tried to rationalize my lack of insurance was that one of my closest friends is a surgeon, so if I felt a cold coming on or thought I'd punctured an organ, I could just text her things like: MY SIDE HURTS—AM I DYING? or MY EYE WAS JUST TWITCHING! ANEURYSM? Another way I rationalized it was by giving myself mental pep talks about how evil insurance companies are and how I shouldn't have to pay them all this money just to go to the doctor once a year. But that's not rebellious or cool—it's just ridiculous. I don't adore health insurance companies or pharmaceutical giants, but I bet I would have liked them just a tiny bit if I'd found myself in the hospital during that time, which I almost did.

A few months after I was laid-off, I was in a minor fender bender and wound up with a tweaked back, a black eye, and a weird pain in my side that I self-diagnosed as a punctured kidney that was going to kill me in my sleep. This led to more frantic texts to my surgeon friend: HOW CAN I TELL IF MY KIDNEY IS PUNCTURED?? She finally, understandably, got fed up with me and replied, GO TO THE HOSPITAL AND FIND OUT.

Let me tell you, when you're feeling that kind of pain, a quart-sized bottle of Advil and a marathon of *Fashion Police* will not cure you. Joan Rivers was funny, but she was no orthopedist, and searching WebMD will only convince you that the minor cut on your hand is the beginning of a flesh-eating bacteria and you should immediately begin writing your will. WebMD is not an actual, living, breathing MD, which is sometimes hard to remember. I was extremely lucky that I didn't actually puncture a kidney, and, if I had, I would have been cursing my insurance-less ass to this day, because I would probably still be paying the bill.

WebMD is not an actual, living, breathing MD, which is sometimes hard to remember.

Health insurance is a very serious topic. Your health is a very serious topic. So don't be an idiot like me, and like my brother from another mother, the $1 bank robber. At least he had a plan—I was just being an asshole. Work health insurance into your budget—call several companies, compare rates, try to negotiate (remember—haggling is your friend). And, whatever you do, do not try and self-diagnose by Googling your symptoms. You'll just convince yourself you have fifteen incurable diseases, bed bugs, a brown recluse spider bite, malaria, restless leg syndrome, and bubonic plague. You'll get so worked up that you'll actually make yourself sick . . . and then you'll really wish you had insurance.

12

DON'T SELL YOUR ORGANS—
YOU NEED THOSE!

During college, my friends and I were more concerned with passing our Archaeology of Chiefdoms tests than we were with calculating how many eggs our bodies were producing. Soothing articles like "Women Lose 90 Percent of their Eggs by 30!!!" and "If You Don't Have Kids by 25 You're Screwed" weren't as common then, so we lived in a bit of a bubble. Eggs were the things you shoved into your piehole to help you forget your raging hangover. We didn't know our ovarian stock was plummeting as we ate our breakfast burritos. Those were the glory days. Ignorance was definitely bliss, even if we did have pounding headaches.

Toward the end of college, ads started popping up in the back of the school paper and in the city weekly urging, DONATE YOUR EGGS. The word "donate" sounds so pleasant and selfless, as if you're handing a fistful of dandelions and some canned soup to an elderly beggar. They were offering thousands of dollars in the ads, which is a fortune to a college student who is earning peanuts waiting tables at Yum Yum Dim Sum or making minimum wage as a teaching assistant. The ads became a big topic of conversation. I knew of one sorority girl who actually went through with it. Her personality was as lively as a Styrofoam cup, so we didn't really get any details about the procedure from her. We just got, "It was fine. I don't know. Whatever." Riveting stuff.

Please note that selling your organs is not the same as donating an organ to help save someone's life. Please also note that I know eggs aren't technically an organ. They're . . . eggs, I guess. I would never tell someone what to do with his or her body—unless it was my child and he or she wanted to get a giant bicep tattoo of Rush Limbaugh. Barring that, your body is your own, and it's none of my business what you do with it. But I'll just state for the record that I don't think you should sell your eggs or any of your organs unless you have contemplated the consequences long and hard—and by that I mean for several months, if not a year. You might need those organs. Plus, it's kind of a creepy procedure. Would you sell your spleen? No. Would you auction off your aorta? Doubt it. It's not like selling your reproductive stock entails popping into a clinic, having a doctor wave a magic wand until a few eggs float into a container, and skipping out into the sunshine to go cash your $8,000 check. What it does entail is thorough background checks (which is fine, unless you're a double agent), mental health evaluations, hormone shots, multiple ultrasounds, and then . . . the procedure. Possibly followed by excruciating cramps. When you read up on it, they use the word "harvesting" a lot, which sounds more "dystopian sci-fi horror movie" and less "planting peony seeds in the garden." Or maybe that's just me.

There are plenty of people who could benefit from egg donors, so if it makes you feel good to be part of that, then maybe it's worth it. Just don't make it a hasty decision. Give it months of thought before deciding that financially, emotionally, and physically, it's the right decision for you.

On the other hand, if it's a rash decision and it's purely for extra money so you can go to South Beach for spring break or buy a Van Cleef & Arpels sapphire bird pendant, there are plenty of other options: wait tables, temp, babysit, tutor, kick ass in whatever job you're doing and ask for a raise; work in tech support or retail; or become a personal trainer, barista, bank teller, Pilates teacher, rodeo clown, or ventriloquist. I understand that to make $8,000 as a barista takes a long time. Personally I'd rather serve frittatas for tips than donate my eggs. It might not be a quick way to make a few grand, but at least you're not being "harvested."

And if you're a dude and you want to make some extra cash by selling some sperm, knock yourself out. You guys don't have to read scary articles about your sperm count drying up like a jellyfish in the Sahara once you hit "a certain age." You can hand that stuff out like Halloween candy until the day you die—or at least until you're in your seventies or something. Lucky you.

Like I said, it's your body. Just make sure you're making a wise, not rash, financial decision when it comes to selling organs, limbs, and bodily fluids of any kind. It's not like you're selling a busted Panini maker or some throwaway body part like an appendix. Just give it some thought.

13

IT'S NOT JUST A COFFEE SHOP.
IT'S AN EXPERIENCE.

n some parts of the world, people just pop some coffee beans in their mouths and chew. Cowboys used to boil water over a fire, throw in some grounds, pour the boiling black liquid into a tin cup, and gulp it down as they contemplated the trail ahead or the saloon girl they loved or whatever it was old-timey cowboys thought about. Horses? Poker games? Lassoes? Snake bites? Bacon? Smallpox? Syphilis? Sarsaparilla? Cowboys didn't have the luxury of ordering a Grande Soy Vanilla Latte. They were too busy worrying about getting gored by bulls to wait around for perfect foam with leaf patterns in their drinks.

Most of us aren't cowboys, so we do occasionally like to get fancy coffee drinks with leaf patterns swirled into the foam. Lots of financial gurus tell you that you will save a ton of money if you stop buying $5 lattes every day, and that's true. If you're forking over five bucks a day, seven days a week, you're spending $1,825 on coffee a year, and $9,125 over five years—and that's for just *one* coffee a day. That might not be a make-or-break number for you, but if it is, you need to get a tin cup and light a campfire, or just get a Mr. Coffee coffeemaker or a French press. If $1,000 a year will chip away at your student-loan bill or help pay for that health insurance you need, then find a way to spend less on coffee and use the rest of it for bills. I'm not saying that curbing your coffee habit will make you rich. It's a cup of coffee you're giving up, not fifteen Bulgari necklaces. But it can help you spend more wisely and make room for more important expenses. Although coffee is pretty important.

It's not so bad making coffee at home. Sometimes, though, you're busy or you need to treat yourself and you just want an overpriced latte made by a skinny man in skinny jeans. The first time I went to Intelligentsia, a very posh-but-pretending-it's-not coffee bar in Los Angeles, I waited in line with a friend while engaging in my favorite pastime—eavesdropping and silently psychoanalyzing everyone around me. One of the guys in line must have been an Intelligentsia novice too, because I saw his buddy lean in and reverently declare:

If $1,000 a year will chip away at your student-loan bill or help pay for that health insurance you need, then find a way to spend less on coffee and use the rest of it for bills.

"It's not just a coffee shop. It's an experience."

If I'd had coffee in my mouth at that very moment, I would have spit it all over that bombastic guy's bespoke overalls. What the hell was he talking about? It looked like "just a coffee shop" to me. There weren't any roller coasters or virtual reality rooms. I didn't see anyone morphing into a superhero or streaking through the streets because the magical caffeine coursing through their veins was teleporting them to another dimension. My friend and I silently telegraphed our disdain back and forth via our eyeballs as the dude in the overalls preached the gospel of coffee and by osmosis made everyone around him just a little more pompous. Myself included.

With pretention accosting us from every angle, we waited in line another twenty minutes. We're human, and that means that when another human says that something is so amazing it will change your life, you need to find out for yourself whether or not they're full of shit. If it was an "experience," I wanted it.

We eventually shuffled inside and got our overpriced coffee, which the baristas individually brew with tender loving care. It was delicious—creamy and perfect and strong. Still, it was a cup of coffee. It's not like we drank it and immediately had an earth-shattering epiphany for every dollar we spent. When the last sip was gulped and we tossed our recyclable paper cups into the trash-can, I realized that it was just a coffee shop, and the "experience" that guy was talking about must be the moment you get the bill and realize that you just caved and spent $5 on a cup of coffee. Not a latte or macchiato or Frappuccino Mocha Latte with hazelnut soy—a cup of coffee. Technically, the annoyance and disbelief you experience when you look at the bill could be considered an epiphany, but it's not a very good one.

If you're reading this right now, you're probably not a gun-slinging, cow-herding cowboy circa 1840. Chances are, you're living in the twenty-first century, and you want to buy a fancy coffee now and then. If that's the case, go for it. You don't need to gnaw on coffee grinds to save money, but you should think long-term about your finances, whether that involves a 401(k), life insurance, or $5 lattes, 365 days a year, in perpetuity. Let's look at the numbers again:

Total annual expenditure for $5 daily lattes

1 year	5 years	10 years
$1,825	$9,125	$18,250

And that's not even accounting for inflation. Like stepping away from lotto tickets, forgoing coffee will not make you rich. But curbing your excess coffee spending will, obviously, help you save money, and it'll also help you spend that money on more necessary expenses if you really need to. It's more about trimming the fat than depriving yourself. Plus, wouldn't you rather take that cash and buy a home or go on a trip to Argentina or Portugal or Paraguay? You can get amazing coffee in all those places, and it'll be a hell of a lot more interesting than buying yet another Frappuccino, as far as life experiences go.

14

LIVING LARGE IN
THE CHEAP SEATS

C ulture is wonderful, but it's not always cheap. When you're on a budget it may seem frivolous to spend $50 to see Tuvan throat singers perform in a ballroom, $400 on Coachella tickets, or $200 to see *The Book of Mormon*, but there are ways to get out of the house and experience some culture, even if you're in the cheap seats, which are better than no seats at all.

And now get ready, because here comes a one-question pop quiz that will require all of your brainpower to answer.

You know those fabulous people with interesting shoes who are always gushing about the symphony or the latest art installation piece that really exemplified the juxtaposition of this or that? To be cultured like them you need to:

A. Be a multimillionaire

B. Have a friend who is a multimillionaire

C. Become a celebrity

D. Be curious, hungry for culture, and resourceful

The answer is D, although C certainly wouldn't hurt. You don't need to be part of Leonardo DiCaprio's entourage to enjoy the theater or a VIP art opening or an NBA game once in a while. Plus, if front-row seats aren't in the cards, sitting farther back isn't so bad. Expanding your mind in the nosebleed section is better than becoming one with the couch and watching *Mama's Family* reruns all weekend. Culture and art feed your soul and make you smarter, and when you're smarter you can get better jobs, which lead to more money and better seating options.

Not all cities are overflowing with cultural events. Maybe you're in Plain City, Utah (population 5,887), or Tomball, Texas (population 10,964), and the chances of a Broadway show coming to town are slim to no-way-in-hell. Don't get discouraged. Every town has something to offer. Tomball's official website lists: tearooms, country cooking, honky tonkin', ice cream hand-dipped by real soda jerks, and the Rails & Tails Mudbug Festival. I actually think a mudbug festival sounds pretty fun. If you've just written me off as a maniac, you should know that "mudbugs" are also known as crawfish, crawdads, and—for the true optimists out there—freshwater lobsters. The point is, when exploring cultural opportunities, it's paramount that you keep an open mind about things like mudbugs, soda jerks, and honky tonkin'.

Whether you're stuck in a tiny hellhole of a town or living it up in an exciting, vibrant metropolis, there are ways to get your culture free and/or cheap. Let's look at a few.

Art Galleries. Most cities and towns have art galleries, and if you scour the papers or the Internet for openings, you can find your weekends filled with free beer and wine and culture. You might have to listen to people say things like, "The sublime deconstruction of form overshadows the inherent specificity of her oeuvre," but don't let bullshit art talk like that stop you. You might not get what they're saying, but I can guarantee you that they don't either. Art galleries are always fun, no matter how lame the paintings are or how many times you have to hear the word "oeuvre." Plus, free wine.

Street Fairs. Every place has its own version of a mudbug festival. The fests are usually free, or they have a small fee of five or ten bucks. Whether it's a Grilled Cheese Fest, Vintage Motorcycle Day, or a Bluegrass Music Festival, get out of the house and check them out. If you don't like it, you don't ever have to go back.

Free Museum Days. If there's a museum in your town, chances are they offer free admission once a week or once a month. Take advantage of their generosity. Go stare at Picassos or Liberace memorabilia or Greek sculptures or all the variations of barbed wire you can handle. I've been to a barbed wire museum in Texas and, let me tell you, it was pretty fun. There are a lot of variations of barbed wire out there: Crandall Zigzag, Upham's Snail, Brinkerhoff Twisted Ribbon, Scutt Split Arrow Plate barb. See—culture!

Outdoor Theater/Concerts. If you see the words "free" and "concert" next to each other, it's pretty much a no-brainer. Even if it's a Willow and Jaden Smith variety show or an Ace of Base reunion tour—you might be in agony, but at least you won't be home alone wondering what people in the outside world are doing. Plus, some theaters and concert halls will offer half-price same-day tickets—so if you're the spontaneous type, it's worth looking into.

University Events. If there's a college nearby, they likely have a theater department, an art department, and a dance department. See if they have any free or cheap performances going on. In 2014, the College of Southern Idaho staged productions of *Oedipus Tyrannus*, *Antigone* (one of my personal faves—she was such a rebel), the complete works of Shakespeare (abridged), and Robert Anderson's *I Never Sang For My Father*. There's some highbrow shit going on in places like Twin Falls. So—no excuses.

Gardens. Strolling through a Japanese garden and contemplating a giant lily pad is a cultural activity, in my opinion. Depending on what time of year you go, botanical gardens offer cherry blossoms (*Prunus serrullata*), Chinese Snowballs (*Viburnum macrocephalum*), and Japanese gardens with moon bridges and koi ponds for some decent entry fees; there might even be a free one near you. Just don't go trampling through a neighbor's garden to get your flora on, unless they chopped down your sycamore tree and you're out for revenge.

Lectures. The word "lecture" might give you painful flashbacks to high school physics class, but try to remain calm. I once saw a lecture on earthquakes given by a badass lady seismologist while I was sipping wine at the Natural History Museum, and, although I had my doubts at first, it was a pretty cool way to spend a Friday. Libraries, universities, community centers, and bookstores often offer free or cheap lectures on topics like art history, 1970s cinema, Balinese cooking, and everybody's favorite—natural disasters.

Go on a Walk. There are few activities that are cheaper than walking around and staring at things. Get lost in your town and discover new hidden gems, or print out some "Haunted Places of Baton Rouge" list you found online and learn about your local ghosts with some friends. I've done a "Hidden staircases of Los Angeles" walking tour, and it was pretty interesting. It's not a bad way to spend a Sunday, plus it's free. And you're walking up and down stairs, which counts as a workout.

Lucha Libre. Culture doesn't always have to be about going to the symphony or the Louvre. It can be about watching men in glittery masks and capes catapulting themselves onto opponents and then pretending to strangle them with their thigh muscles. Or maybe you should get out of your comfort zone and get tickets to a monster truck rally (tickets to the Monster Jam range from $25 for basic seats to $60 for VIP and $70 for front row). Who doesn't want to watch a 9,000-pound truck with six-foot tires and names like *Raminator* or *Monster Mutt Dalmatian* fly through the air?

City Council Meeting. I can think of few activities that seem more mind-numbing and soul-squashing than a city council meeting, but if you're truly desperate—or if you get off listening to people drone on about potholes and sewage contracts—knock yourself out. Maybe you'll make some friends, get fired up about amending the library's late-fee policy, or decide to get into politics and run for office. Stranger things have happened in the political arena, as you obviously already know.

If your town really is so small that none of these activities exist, I suggest you appoint yourself Cultural Ambassador, team up with some like-minded friends, and get some lectures and street fairs and amateur film festivals rolling. I'm not suggesting that you run out and look for seed money and form an LLC, but you can do it on a small scale. Like in your garage. Chances are, closet painters and sculptors and seismologists will start coming out of the woodwork. Good luck with that.

15

WHAT'S SO FUNNY ABOUT TAXES? NOTHING. SO LET'S JUST GET THIS OVER WITH

When tax time rolls around, I head straight to the back room of a rinky-dink hair salon, late at night, under cover of darkness. That little rundown room in the back of Joie de Vivre Hair & Waxing is where my "tax lady," as I like to call her, does her thing. From what I can tell, she punches numbers into a calculator and eats greasy Chinese takeout as I sit and stare and silently grapple with philosophical questions like:

1. Why didn't I become an accountant?
2. What is wrong with me?
3. How much self-doubt can you have when your career involves a calculator?

Watching someone do your taxes is a real bore—it helps if you can entertain yourself.

I don't love dealing with taxes, but, like voting, it makes me feel a little patriotic. I'm sure any libertarians reading this just experienced a pulmonary embolism, but I don't know what to tell you guys. That's just how I feel. Would I rather not pay taxes? Of course—I'm not (completely) insane. But we all know what happens to people who avoid paying taxes. They get thrown in the pokey, the slammer, the hoosegow. Translation: they're screwed. They wear baggy, unflattering jumpsuits day after day, and they wind up paying more than they actually owed. And, as is the case with kleptos, nobody likes them. Where's the freedom and glamour in that?

Besides imbuing me with a vague sense of patriotism, tax day also makes me imagine some dude in a tie-dyed shirt living off the grid and slinging back tequila shots in a Mexican dive bar. He's either avoiding paying taxes or avoiding getting arrested for the fifteen human heads he left hidden in a basement back home in Nebraska. Whatever the reason, every April this phantom hippie murderer pops into my mind, perhaps as a way to warn me that the alternative to not paying taxes isn't pretty. It's riddled with guilt, smells of cheap Mezcal, and wears worn T-shirts with catchy slogans like: IF YOU MEET A WOMAN WHO WILL WASH YOUR TRUCK—MARRY HER. I guess that's my psyche's way of keeping me calm and cool when my tax lady finishes poking her calculator and shows me the numbers. I just think of that tie-dye-wearing, tax-evading serial killer and think, "Well, at least I'm not *that* guy." Maybe I should have gone into psychology, because that is some next-level, science-of-the-mind shit right there. I highly recommend you give it a try.

If you're working, you need to pay taxes. You can go cry to your momma about it, but it's simply a fact, so deal with it. You can use online programs like TurboTax, but once I started paying an actual human to do my taxes, I never went back. While you could fork over a ton of money for this, you can also find people who are legit but cheap like my Joie de Vivre tax lady. The reason I'd rather pay someone to do my taxes is that I don't have an accountant-type brain. Whatever the polar opposite of an accountant-type brain looks like, that's the mental ticker I was dealt. I can do basic math and add and subtract fractions (at least, I think I can still add and subtract fractions), but I'm paralyzed by fear when I see a jar of jellybeans with a sign reading GUESS THE NUMBER! That game is barbaric. I know that W-2s don't have a ton in common with jellybeans, but if you can relate, I highly recommend you find someone of your own and spare yourself the agony.

Whether you pay someone to do your taxes or you take them on yourself, there are a few things you can do throughout the year to make it easier come March or April. You can keep a Word doc listing any expenses you think you might forget. Keep track of your mileage to and from work, and to and from any work-related events. If you take the subway to work, keep track of all those fares. If you bought a new car, that's a write-off. If you had to buy a new wardrobe for work, same deal. That little server apron you hate? Keep the receipt. Each industry has specific things that are legal to write off, so ask around, do some research, and find out exactly what you can deduct each year.

For example, if you work in entertainment, you can write off a portion of any entertainment-related expenses you spent for your job. If you write about TV and are required to know about every show on cable, Hulu, and Netflix, you can write off those payments. If you're a professional dog sitter, you can deduct things like treats and leashes. If you run your business from home, you can deduct a portion of your rent and any project supplies you bought.

During the year, make sure you keep all your receipts physically or digitally or both so you don't forget, because you will, unless you have the brainpower of Nikola Tesla. I keep my receipts in a Ziploc bag, which isn't very fancy or dignified, but the thought of scrolling through an entire year of bank and credit card transactions online sounds miserable to me. I'd rather put on some music, sit on my floor, and un-crinkle a wad of receipts for an hour. Call me old-fashioned, call me a Luddite—I don't mind. It works for me; you should find the system that works for you. Maybe you want to digitally alphabetize and color code your receipts throughout the year—be my guest. I happen to prefer the Ziploc-bag method. It's foolproof and technology-free.

If you're a freelancer whose checks have no taxes deducted, you might feel rich(ish), but please, whatever you do, save a portion of each check, because you will have to pay a chunk of change come tax time. The IRS doesn't take pity on freelancers. They don't take pity on anyone, really. Bureaucratic cyborgs seldom do, so be prepared.

And don't try and pull one over on the good old IRS. They'll hunt you down, eventually. It might take them a few years to dig themselves out from under the reams of paperwork they're buried beneath, but eventually, somehow, they will come along in their brown suits and rubber-soled shoes and ask what in the world you donated to Goodwill back in 2013 that was worth $5,000. When it comes to taxes, just be honest. Or else you can head on down to Mexico like the phantom hippie murderer in my head, become a Mezcal aficionado, and never look back. That is, until they come down and cuff you. If that seems ludicrous, that our government would spend much-needed funds sending agents to another country to nab someone who lied about his or her taxes or income, take note: a wily broad named Wanda Lee Ann Podgurski was arrested in Mexico in 2013 for fraud after she taunted a district attorney by tweeting CATCH ME IF YOU CAN. And they did.

III.

HOME

The ornament of a house is the friends who frequent it.
—Ralph Waldo Emerson

*We're going to inlay the floors with a lot of onyx
and amethyst and semi-precious stones.*
—Jackie Siegel, a.k.a. the "Queen of Versailles"[6]

---

6. Pressler, Jessica. "177 Minutes With Jackie Siegel." *New York Magazine* 26 Apr 2013 http://nymag.com/news/intelligencer/encounter/jackie-siegel-2013-5/.

16

WHO NEEDS A HOUSE WHEN
YOU CAN LIVE IN YOUR HONDA

O wning a home is the American dream. If you live in Manhattan
or San Francisco or Los Angeles, owning an actual home with
a yard and space—as opposed to owning a sixth-floor walk-up
that's roughly the size of an acorn—is another thing altogether.
It's way beyond the *Little House on the Prairie* days where owning
some land and a wooden house with a roof and a working chimney
was considered pretty stellar. In the twenty-first century, Charles
and Caroline and Laura Ingalls would be considered bonnet-wear-
ing bums. Well, Charles didn't exactly wear a bonnet. He had that
thick, wavy 1970s do, which maybe added some sex appeal to the
show. He was the Fabio of family television, and a homeowner
to boot.

In major cities today, walking past big, beautiful homes probably doesn't make you go, "Look honey, it's the American dream."
You're probably more like, "God-fucking-damnit, who the hell are
these people? How does anyone afford this? Screw real estate, I'm
moving to Toledo!" Actually, if you really want a house, cities like
Toledo and Detroit might be the way to go. When I drive around

Los Angeles and cruise past gorgeous homes with little rainbows shimmering across their rolling green lawns, due to the fact that the California sun is hitting the perfectly arching streams of sprinkler water just so, I don't immediately think, "Someday, I, too, will have a lawn full of rainbows!" Instead, the first thing that pops into my head is, "Their water bill must be insane." I don't know if that makes me cynical or cheap or so practical that I deserve a medal. The answer probably depends on you. I'd like to give myself a medal, so I'll go with the last option, thank you very much.

Maybe you have a house, but you still yearn for a bigger, better home with bay windows, a terrace, and an infinity pool. It's "keeping up with the Joneses" all over again. For your sake, I hope your neighbor isn't Jackie "Queen of Versailles" Siegel, who is building a ninety-thousand-square-foot mansion in Florida with ten kitchens, a roller rink, and a four-thousand-square-foot closet with a gold elevator inside. If the Siegels can afford all of that excess, good for them. But does anyone need ten kitchens? Bobby Flay and Cat Cora are probably both fine with just one. And a gold closet elevator? I mean, come on. That's ten kitchens to clean, multiple toilets to plunge, and ten refrigerators to power. Instead of awarding myself a medal this time around I think I'll crown myself the "Queen of Practicality." It sounds much more regal than "Queen of the Studio Apartments" or "Queen of the Renters."

Obviously Versailles is an extreme example, whether it's in Florida or France. Most of us just want a safe, cozy home to call our own. For some, owning a home feels like a faraway fantasy that will only come true if you win the lotto (if this sounds tempting to you please flip back to chapter 8) or meet a magical genie who grants you three wishes, one of them being, "I would like a mansion and a staff of servants, like on *Downton Abbey* or *The Real Housewives*." Well, listen up because I have some good news for you. You don't need to "get rich quick" to buy a house. Really. You don't even need to get rich.

As an example, let's look at an artist friend of mine who is nowhere near Damien Hirst's tax bracket, but who has managed to buy not one but three properties in and around Los Angeles. Let's call him Sal. His path to becoming a homeowner might sound a little extreme—since not everyone can live in his or her car for five years, shower at the gym, and exist on a diet of Subway sandwiches in order to save up for a house—but it worked for him. Sal decided he wanted to own land, he made a plan, and he moved into his car to save up and make that happen. That's pretty admirable. He didn't rob a bank or become a klepto. He just moved into his Honda Ridgeline.

"The best advice I can give is: you better work," he says. "Those years of living in the truck, which I enjoyed and thought of as 'urban camping,' have now yielded three properties. Start small and work up if you're broke." Take that, Tony Robbins.

Here's another tip: Sal "took lovers" when it was especially cold or rainy so he didn't have to shiver in the truck as water leaked onto his face, so there were nights during that time when he had a roof over his head. It takes a lot of stamina (and some would say mania) to do what he did, but he's living proof that it is possible to become a homeowner even if you're not "rich." You might just have to move into your car for a few years and take lovers to make it happen. That, my friends, is the American dream. If you have the stamina to make it happen, godspeed and good luck. If not, just work really hard and hope to hell the cost of housing goes down.

17

THE PERKS OF BEING A RENTER

Say the whole five-years-in-the-truck-taking-lovers-and-eating-Subway scenario isn't working for you. You're a renter. You're living in a teeny studio that has a teeny kitchen (which means no oven and no freezer), and you're feeling sorry for yourself. Nobody likes a crybaby, so you need to put an end to the pity party right now. There are definitely perks when it comes to renting, and if you're in a funk about your three-hundred-square-foot living quarters, it's time to stop pining for a Spanish colonial mansion and start loving your little casita.

Right this second, I'm sitting in my own studio apartment. Well, it's not technically my own since I have a landlord and thus no legal rights to the place, but whatever. Let me give you the grand tour. When you waltz through the door, you find yourself inside a rectangular space that serves as the bedroom, living room, dining room, den, TV room, home theater, office, library, changing room, closet, gym (more on that later), and bicycle storage space. It's really quite something. Once you've let the grandeur sink in, a foot-long hallway leads you into the kitchen, which is roughly the size of one and a half porta-potties. Here you'll find a mini fridge, cook top, sink, four cabinets, a George Foreman Grill that's covered in dust, some drawers, a window, and a floor. Spectacular! Then, if you pivot to your right, you'll practically be standing in the master bathroom, which is also roughly the size of one and a half porta-potties, shower included. Notice the architectural symmetry at work here. If you walk too far into the loo you'll smash your face on the shower door, so . . . baby steps. Crane your neck to the left and behold the sink, toilet, window, floor, walls, and cabinets. And that, folks, is the end of our tour! I know. It's pretty amazing.

It may be tiny, but I do love my little apartment. It helps that it has wood floors, a really pretty garden area right outside, and quiet, cool neighbors—and it's a fifteen-minute walk to the beach. Would I like to live in a place that has an oven and a freezer one day? Hell yes. But I appreciate my diminutive oasis. Maybe because before this I was living in a tiny, rundown place in Brooklyn that I'm pretty sure was thrown together with tin, Krazy Glue, and cigarette butts. My landlord came over to fix the oven one day (it did have an oven, I'll give it that), and when I opened the door he had a lit cigarette hanging out of his mouth, which he didn't get rid of when he strolled inside to inspect the appliance in question. Since we weren't in a *Mad Men* episode, I found the fact that he waltzed into my (though technically his) space with a lit cigarette pretty depressing twenty-first-century behavior. He obviously didn't give a damn about the place, and he owned it. It really was the pits.

If you're feeling blue about your small apartment, remember that you don't have to pay property taxes, deal with maintenance issues, or stress about whether the value of your house is rising or sinking. Someone else takes care of the yard and the plumbing, and you don't have to pay for it. If you stumble home drunk and pass out in a shrub, the landlord has to deal with the smashed foliage, not you! No freezer? No ice cream binges. And since I don't bake cupcakes, not having an oven doesn't leave me lost in a dark, sugarless abyss. One trick I developed is to think of my place as a "beach bungalow" instead of a "tiny, ovenless rectangle with windows." It really helps. If you live near the mountains, call it your "cabin." If you're in the plains, call it your "homestead." If you're in a crowded, bustling concrete jungle, think of it as your "high-class prison cell." If that doesn't work, think of it as a "roof over your head," which is a nice thing to have no matter where you live.

I would definitely like the option of having ice-cream binges and cooking cupcakes one day. But until then, I will

If you're feeling blue about your small apartment, remember that you don't have to pay property taxes, deal with maintenance issues, or stress about whether the value of your house is rising or sinking.

embrace my beach bungalow and my porta-potty kitchen, and you should too, because someday, when you're writing a check for your property taxes, you might just think back on your thimble-sized cabin/homestead/jail cell and miss the good old days. It's not entirely likely that this will happen, but anything is possible.

18

ISO ROOMMATE: SANITY A PLUS

We chose Arlo because he was the least psychotic person that strolled through our door that weekend. Compared to the twenty-year-old woman who was clinging to her mom's arm and the creepy ponytailed guy who kept opening and closing the freezer door and saying, "I need a really big freezer. This freezer might not be big enough for me . . ." Arlo seemed as wholesome and lovable as a Furby. He did wear Birkenstocks, but when interviewing potential roommates from Craigslist, you pick your battles.

At the time, I was living with my good friend Sasha in a tiny three-bedroom apartment. It had electric blue shag carpet and low ceilings, which gave the place a 1970s dungeon vibe, but it was cheap so we convinced ourselves the décor was "disco eclectic." The two of us could afford it on our own, but the idea of saving a few hundred bucks every month sounded smart, and so we put an ad on Craigslist and endured a parade of lunatics before settling on Arlo. He could hold a conversation, he had good references, he didn't mention the freezer, and he seemed cool. Hippie, but cool.

Once Arlo moved in, I hoped we'd be like Jack, Janet, and Chrissy on *Three's Company*—best buddies hanging out at the Regal

Beagle, talking about our crazy landlord, and maybe doing a pratfall here and there just to mix things up. That didn't happen. Arlo was nice enough, but he was always off camping and eating wheat germ while Sasha and I were smoking cigarettes, drinking wine, and watching David Lynch movies. It helps if you and your roommates have at least some similar interests, but since Arlo was rarely home our wildly different lifestyle choices didn't cause any friction. At least, not at first.

After a few weeks, we noticed that Arlo had one little flaw, which was that he was a filthy, unsanitary slob who behaved as if he'd been reared by wolves or orangutans in the forest, leaving crumbs everywhere and creating an ant infestation. Soon after he moved in, cups, plates, and utensils started disappearing from the kitchen. At first we thought we had a ghost (watching too many David Lynch movies can mess with your mind), but we talked it out and came to the conclusion that ghosts probably have no need for cheap mugs and chipped plates. And then, after we'd exhausted all other possibilities, we looked over at Arlo's closed bedroom door looming next to the kitchen and suddenly it all made sense.

"I'm scared to go in there," Sasha said, and who could blame her? We hadn't seen Arlo's room since he'd moved in, and, judging from his habits in the kitchen, we guessed it wouldn't be a midcentury modern paradise.

"Let's just peek," I said. "I bet he's hoarding all the mugs."

We crept to the door and carefully twisted the knob. Arlo was off camping near Big Sur but we were still scared he might pop up at any moment, like the tiny demonic hologram people in Lynch's *Mulholland Drive*.

I pushed the door open and peeked inside. There was no furniture, and the off-white walls were completely bare. Arlo's decorative style was basically that of a homeless caveman with no flair. Beneath the gigantic pile of clothes and shoes and who knows what else that was taking up the entire floor, we could just make out the edge of a thin mattress with fading blue stripes. And sure enough, as we suspected, Arlo's mound of miscellany was dotted with crusty mugs and plates and spoons, all from our kitchen.

"Disgusting," said Sasha. "I'm not touching that stuff. We'll have to buy all new cups and plates."

We could buy new cups, but we also had to find a way to talk to Arlo about these issues. We didn't want to insult him by starting the conversation off accusing him of being a slob. You should try and discuss issues with your roommates in a calm, rational way because you're inhabiting the same space they are, and it's usually a cramped space, so there's nowhere to run and hide when things get ugly, except your room, the bathtub, or behind the tree on the corner outside.

When Arlo got home from his trip, we casually asked him about all the mugs and plates in the kitchen, since we didn't want him to know we'd been in his room.

"Do you happen to know where all the utensils and plates and cups and glasses are?" I asked. He thought about it for a second, and then a revelatory look came across his face, as if he'd just that second realized he'd been hoarding them all.

"Oh man, you know what? Some of them might be in my room. I'll clean them. It's just a couple. Sorry."

He disappeared into his room, emerged with the evidence, cleaned everything, and put it all back in the cabinets. (I made a mental note of which cups were safe and which cups I would not touch again, since they'd been gathering dust and who knows what else in Arlo's man cave.) We didn't speak of it again and life went back to normal. After a few weeks, though, the crumbs and the ants came back. One day, I cleared the crumbs off the counter (silently cursing Arlo and his parents, who obviously taught him nothing about life, self-respect, and cleanliness), and I baked my first-ever blueberry pie, which was totally out of character but you do crazy shit in your twenties so what can I say. The pie was gorgeous, and I stood back and admired it for a while since the best dessert I'd cooked previously was two Nilla Wafers with peanut butter in the middle, like a sandwich. Basking in my accomplishment, I decided to wait and have a piece of my creation with Sasha later that night while we watched *Lost Highway* for the tenth time, and I left a note for Arlo telling him that I made a pie and that he was welcome to have a piece. And then I went to run some errands.

When I came home later that day, I walked inside to a horrific site, and it wasn't the electric blue shag carpet. On the kitchen counter sat my once-beautiful blueberry pie, surrounded by crumbs, entirely eaten except for one measly piece. It looked pitiful, and there was only one roommate to blame—unless Sasha was going through some kind of crisis she hadn't told me about.

You can't really kick someone out of the apartment because they ate a fruit pie you made. I mean, you can, but you'd be a real asshole. After a quick conversation, Sasha was cleared of the charges, and I asked Arlo about the incident, but he inflated my ego so much by saying how good it was that I let it go. It was my first blueberry pie, so his flattery went a long way.

It wasn't enough though. The final straw with Arlo happened on a summer day, when Sasha came bursting into my room, yelling, "He's keeping a bottle of pee in the bathtub!"

She had to share a bathroom with him because we'd flipped a coin before Arlo came on board to see who would get the small bedroom with its own bathroom and who would get the "big" bedroom and have to share the bathroom with the new guy. Sasha, a true germaphobe right up there with Howard Hughes, saw her worst nightmare come true when the coin landed on "tails" that day.

"He's gross, but he's not hoarding urine, Sasha. Why would he? To wash his hair?"

"I don't know, but I know it's pee! I can't share a bathroom with him anymore. It's so gross. I can't. I can't!"

"It's probably shampoo," I said, imagining that if Arlo did actually use shampoo, it would probably resemble piss.

"It's not. I'm telling you. Think about it."

Sasha was so worked up that I did something that to this day I cannot believe I did, just to shut her up.

"Look, I'll smell it. I'm sure it's shampoo, and if I'm right, will you calm down?" I didn't think about what would happen if I was wrong.

Sasha agreed and I followed her into the bathroom.

"There!" she said, pointing to a clear, unmarked plastic bottle on the side of the tub as if it were a microfiche in a 1970s spy movie. Sure enough, the bottle was filled with a yellowish liquid. Like skydiving or jumping off a cliff into the ocean, this was one of those situations that's best approached with no thought or analysis whatsoever. I walked straight to the bottle, opened the cap, braced myself, and took a big whiff.

"So?! What is it? Is it urine?! It's urine. God! It's Arlo's piss!" Sasha had already turned her back to me and was covering her face with her hands.

"Sasha," I said.

"What?!"

"It's not pee."

She slowly turned to face me again.

"How?"

"It's soap. Or shampoo. I think it's Dr. Bronner's. Probably peppermint. But it's not a urine sample." If it had been what Sasha said it was, I'd probably be running down the street screaming and sobbing and looking for a body of water to jump into, but under the circumstances I felt pretty heroic.

We didn't bring up the incident when Arlo got home and crept into his lair. I mean, how would you bring something like that up? "I just happened to be smelling your shampoo that we thought was piss but it's not, so—congratulations and let's watch a movie!"

A month later, Arlo told us that he was moving in with his girlfriend, and we pretended to be bummed but silently rejoiced. We'd never met this mysterious girlfriend, but I figured that she had probably been raised by wolves as well. For weeks we'd been thinking of ways to ask Arlo to move out but it just seemed so cruel. But then he did it for us. We didn't look for a third roommate after that because the experience had freaked us out about living with anyone we'd met off Craigslist. It also taught us that if we did ever bring in another roommate, we would ask them about their cleaning habits, make a set of chores for each of us to do every week ("clean crumbs" being of the utmost importance), and make sure our lifestyles were at least a tiny bit similar, because wheat germ and wine don't mix.

When you're looking for roommates, you might want to take some of the following tips into consideration so you don't wind up with an Arlo:

Use Craigslist as a last resort. I know people who have found great roommates on Craigslist, but it's rare. First try word of mouth, ask friends and coworkers, post on Facebook, and then, if you're desperate and out of options, go the Craigslist route. And if any potential candidates seem weirdly interested in the size of your freezer, rule them out immediately. #SerialKiller

Set rules. If Sasha and I had sat down with Arlo and talked about cleanliness and crumbs right off the bat . . . he probably still would have been a slob but at least we could have said we tried. Talk to your roommates about expectations, draw up a list of chores and rotate who does what each week (sweeping, trash, dishes, cleaning the toilet—gross). If you have to wake up at dawn for work and your roommate works nights, figure out the noise situation so you're not yelling at each other at two in the morning and waking up the neighbors.

Your best friends could be your worst roommates. Some good friends work out great as roommates, and Sasha and I were a prime example of that. It doesn't always work out that way, though. Before I lived with her I was sharing a two-bedroom apartment with one of my closest friends; while we were like Tweedledum and Tweedledee normally, as roommates we were like Elton John and Madonna, Anthony Bourdain and Paula Deen, Kanye and Taylor Swift—in other words, mortal enemies. Who can explain this phenomenon? It just happens. You won't know until you actually become roommates, which really sucks, but if it's hurting your friendship it's best to quickly try and remedy the situation so you can go back to being buddies, instead of transforming into nemeses.

Beware of significant others. This is also a tough one. Say you have a great roommate and you guys go to movies, get pizza on a Tuesday night, and make each other dinner every other Sunday. Then let's say they get into a serious relationship and suddenly there's this other person eating your food, using your paper towels, and sprawling out on your couch watching *Love & Hip Hop Atlanta* every single night even though they're not paying rent and they have a place of their own. Don't go lock yourself in your room and stew and skip out on pizza night because of all the rage boiling inside you. Talk to your roommate. Ask if they can hang out at their girlfriend/boyfriend's place a few nights a week. Tell them you'd appreciate it if their lover brought over some paper towels once in a while. Little things like that go a long way.

Once you live on your own, you'll rejoice and do as you please and wonder how you ever tolerated roommates. Until that day, choose wisely, communicate calmly, and approach Craigslist with extreme caution. That's one realm where a little paranoia can go a long way.

FLEA MARKET CHIC

There are two kinds of people in this world: those who go antiquing, and those who root around at flea markets and dig through stacks of old creepy dolls, rusty keys, and used saddle shoes in hopes of finding a tin sign from the 1940s advertising motor oil or Morton Salt. But wait! There's a third kind of person. The kind who wouldn't be caught dead buying anything that wasn't brand-new. These people think flea markets are actually full of fleas. Damn: there's a fourth kind of person. The egalitarian, open-minded type who goes antiquing *and* goes rooting through flea markets for gems. Basically, the world is a wondrous melting pot full of many kinds of people with differing, unique, and totally valid feelings about flea markets. Amen.

My earliest feelings about flea markets were fiercely negative, and it wasn't because I was afraid of getting eaten alive by disgusting, blood-sucking parasites. It was because of my mom. Her passion (besides her grandchildren, who she is obsessed with) is interior design. She started dragging me to flea markets when I was in junior high school, and, as you probably know, doing anything with your parents at that time in life is akin to being locked inside a heinous torture chamber of shame, humiliation, and agony. I guess I had nothing else to do, so on weekends we'd drive around Houston hitting up her favorite spots. "Why do we have to do this?!" I'd whine as she drove out to Old Katy Road, home to a giant warehouse full of fading photographs, decaying military medals, and busted-up typewriters. "This is so boring, and everything is so old, just like you!" I was never actually that mean to my mom, but I did come pretty close on a few exceptionally hormonal occasions.

"Honey, you can find some really neat things here, and there are all those old books." I did like the old books; she had me there. Since I knew I was her prisoner for the next few hours, I'd eventually give in and root around in the piles of old jewelry and quilts and antique lace dresses that were so delicate and fragile they looked like they'd turn to dust if you handled them too rough. I don't know what would compel someone to tussle with a pretty, wilting Edwardian gown, but it takes all kinds, as they say. Plus, some of the people you see wandering around flea markets do look a little unhinged, so it's not totally ludicrous to imagine one of them sucker punching an old Victorian slip.

One weekend, out of the blue, my mom turned philosophical as we were strolling through the flea market food court, which smelled like stale popcorn, mothballs, varnish, and BBQ, and which was filled with a lot of people in the three-hundred- to four-hundred-pound range contemplating their leftover pork ribs and jumbo-sized Dr. Peppers. "You know what I like to do sometimes?" she asked cryptically. The woman has a knack for luring you into every thought that passes through her mind by making it sound like she's about to recite Martin Luther King's "I Have a Dream" speech. "What?" I said as bitchily as I possibly could. I pretended I could not have been less interested.

"I like to think about who owned all these things before, what their lives were like, who they loved, what the stories are behind everything."

What the hell? Damn our parents for sometimes saying deep and meaningful things and not always being the clueless, out-of-touch ogres we need them to be so we can act like little assholes and discover our own identities and mature into the unique snowflakes we aspire to become. "Yeah," was all I said as we left the food court. We entered the area where all the rusty tin advertising signs were displayed. Suddenly those Squadron Leader tobacco ads didn't seem so boring or lame. I didn't tell my mom that until years later, of course.

All those tin signs and afternoons on Old Katy Road taught me that scouring flea markets is an economical, fun way to decorate your place with things that no one else will have. It's the opposite of IKEA and Pottery Barn. Those places have some great, practical stuff, but it's nice to mix it up. You need to approach a flea market with an open mind and an endless well of patience. It's not a Quickie Mart. But it is a great place to try out your haggling skills. It's perfectly acceptable to get a few bucks knocked off that beat-up metal mailbox you're planning to plant flowers in, or those vintage tennis rackets you're dying to hang on the entry hall wall. Haggling is part of the fun. Used to be, words like "vintage" meant "old and reasonably priced," but unfortunately, today vintage usually means "precious and rare and expensive as hell." When decorating your home, watch out for red flags like "shabby chic" or "reclaimed." They sound down-home, but they're dangerous.

You need to approach a flea market with an open mind and an endless well of patience. It's not a Quickie Mart.

Unless commissioning someone to design a customized interior for your private jet is in the cards, you should also be cautious when taking your cues from a magazine like *Architectural Digest*. I love reading it, but it's sometimes just as hilarious as *The Onion*. It can be your inspiration, but don't start feeling like you need Louis XVI–style gilt-wood fauteuils[7] or Fabergé frames. If those things are in your budget, knock yourself out, but flea market chic is more

---

7. fau·teuil [FOE-till]: a fancy upholstered armchair. Maybe you already knew what it was. I had to Google it.

about looking for affordable, unique gems than it is about decorating your house like Mary Astor or Mark Zuckerberg.

My mom, the Obi-Wan of flea markets, has found everything from a piece of Baccarat crystal to a stuffed snake with a stuffed rat halfway in its mouth. She bought the crystal, not the snake. Over the years I've picked up a tattered and beautiful copy of *A Child's Garden of Verses* by Robert Louis Stevenson, a 1950s periwinkle blue chiffon party dress, and a vintage Japanese vase with purple irises painted on it—plus paintings, decorative plates, old-timey suitcases (which, when stacked, can double as a table), and, last but not least, a ton of coral and turquoise jewelry when I was going through my "Native American phase" in tenth grade. I'm not proud that I wore moccasins, peg-legged jeans, and layers of turquoise jewelry to school. I guess I just felt connected to the Comanche and Apache tribes we were learning about in history class. But the phase happened, there's nothing I can do about it, and I only have myself to blame. The jewelry was pretty great, though, and I have the flea market to thank for that.

And so, moccasins aside, the moral of the story is: be patient when combing through flea markets, because for every fifteen stuffed snakes you see, you might find one piece of Baccarat crystal; don't feel pressured to spend a fortune and decorate your place with "one-of-a-kind" chandeliers; and accept the fact that sometimes, while walking through a shabby (not chic) food court, your parents just might have something enlightening to say.

20

HOW TO BE A GUILT-FREE GOURMET WHILE PREPPING FOR THE APOCALYPSE

- Packaged beets
- Tiara
- Canned peas
- Salmon jerky
- Granola bar–sized flashlight
- Himalayan sea salt
- Unsweetened applesauce
- Heart-shaped wine stopper
- Nine-inch Torpedo Level
- Birthday candles
- Neon green lighter
- Four-year-old caramels
- Onion soup & dip mix
- Decorative bowl

ehold, my end-of-days stash. I didn't become a survivalist on purpose, but over the years I've made some questionable purchases that just sit in my kitchen cabinets and drawers, gathering dust. I used to feel guilty about these unused items. Packaged beets seemed like a good idea at the time, as did the canned peas, salmon jerky, and unsweetened applesauce. Then, one day, I saw the light. I realized that it's OK to accidentally spend money on disgusting things when you're hormonal or going through a breakup or just really curious about packaged beets, because these things might come in handy during the apocalypse. That was a real revelation: you can prep for Armageddon even if you're on a budget.

The food, lighter, and flashlight (small as it may be) are no-brainers, and you'll find them on any decent survivalist's must-have list. You'll also find guns, ammo, rope, a saw, waterproof matches, and a Hazmat suit, but I'm not vying to win the Best Survivalist of the Year award. I'm just trying to justify my stupid purchases by linking them to the apocalypse, which I suggest you do as well. On that note, I'd like to take a moment to justify some of the more dubious items on my list.

> **Tiara.** Unfortunately, this isn't an ancient heirloom I keep locked away in case I need to offer it to one of those evil humans who become cannibals at the first sign of catastrophe, just in case they want to sprinkle that precious Himalayan sea salt onto my dinky bicep and start gnawing. It's a cheapo tiara that I wore one Halloween when I dressed up as a "bad princess." I know—lame costume. I don't wear it around my beach bungalow or anything; but for whatever reason, the tiara remains in the kitchen drawer. But hear me out: if the earth is scorched and your neighbors are eating each other, wouldn't it lift your spirits and keep you from committing hara-kiri to throw on a plastic tiara or your favorite baseball cap? I think so.

> **Heart-shaped wine stopper.** This isn't sharp enough to use as a weapon, so it serves no real purpose unless I come across a kindly human with some Malbec and we want to put it into the bottle as we sip to remind ourselves that, no matter how hungry we are, and no matter how much we're hallucinating that the other person's left leg is a juicy chicken drumstick—*we are still human.* Only humans use heart-shaped wine stoppers. Its purpose is hope.

Nine-inch Torpedo Level. This might be useful, but I have no idea how to use it. My boyfriend gave it to me one night, which is the only reason I have it. He didn't give it to me wrapped in a bow or anything; he was just rummaging in his junk drawer, and I saw it and asked what it was. "It's a leveler," he said, as if everyone in the world should know such a thing. He pressed it into my palm and told me to take it, because "Everyone should have a leveler." I guess carpenters use it to find out if a surface is even. I'm no carpenter, but if I need to construct a shelter out of roots and twigs and old KFC chicken buckets, I'm sure it will come in handy.

Decorative bowl. I likely won't be throwing any fancy potluck parties to celebrate the end of the world, so using it to hold dip is probably out of the question. Still, I'm pretty sure I'll be able to pop this bowl on top of my head like a helmet if bullets are flying, or use it as a shield if someone starts shooting makeshift BBQ-skewer arrows at me. That, or I can offer it to a cannibal after I've already bartered the tiara.

So you see, even if you're not a millionaire survivalist (or even just a middle-income survivalist), you can prep for the apocalypse. It's also a great way to feel less guilty about your frivolous purchases and unopened carpentry tools. That does not mean you should run out and buy a bunch of things you can't afford and pretend they'll save your life on doomsday. We're talking canned peas here, not Cartier diamonds. Choose wisely.

21

THE FREELOADER'S GUIDE
TO HOUSE-SITTING

Not to sound new-agey or anything, but sometimes the universe really does take care of you. Maybe you get a parking ticket, but a week later you find ten bucks in the street, which will cover about a sixth of your ticket. Or maybe you find out that your boyfriend or girlfriend has been cheating, and a flaming anvil suddenly drops out of the clouds and hits them on the head.

Or maybe, just maybe, you get laid-off, sink into a deep, dark funk that has you zombie-scanning the same tattered copy of *Us Weekly* night and day because looking at photos of Reese Witherspoon taking out the trash makes you feel better, when out of the blue, a Fairy Godperson in the form of an old professor or a home-owning buddy comes to you with these five magical words: Do You Want to House-sit? Those words have healing power. You professional house-sitters out there know exactly what I'm talking about. In my experience, getting house-sitting gigs has been a word-of-mouth kind of thing, but there are online agencies that help place house-sitters, and they work in the same way that agencies for nannies, home chefs, and babysitters work. You create a profile, they make sure you're not a psycho killer, and you can get daily alerts about house-sitting jobs in your area. I would never in a million years pay a stranger to move into my house and make sure it didn't get robbed, but some people are insane, and because of this, you can try and get an anonymous house-sitting gig through a website if the word-of-mouth thing isn't happening.

I was a late bloomer as far as house-sitting goes. My first time was when I was long out of college and had just moved away from the tin-and-cigarette-butt hovel I shared with an ex-boyfriend in Brooklyn. For a few months I stayed with some friends back in Los Angeles, but when I was strong enough to not burst into tears every time I heard Tegan and Sara sing "Call it Off" (which I heard constantly, since I played it every four minutes), I faced the prospect of getting my own place. Jumping into the big, bad world of Los Angeles rentals was daunting, but then a miracle occurred.

"There's a woman in my Pilates class who needs someone to stay at her place in Santa Monica and watch her cats for three months while she goes to work on a movie," my friend Jane told me one night. Her statement doesn't really obliterate any Los Angeles stereotypes people may have, but it was just about the loveliest string of words I'd ever heard. "Yes!" I exclaimed without hesitation. "I'm in!"

"You want to see it first, right?" Jane asked. "I've never been there, and she's kind of odd."

"Yeah, of course, but I definitely want to do it. I need to do it."

This could be called desperation, but I call it a wise financial decision. I would be saving more than $3,000 over the course of three months. You don't have to be a mathematician to calculate the return on that deal.

I didn't know if this woman had two cats or twenty (she had two, thank god), and I didn't know if her place in Santa Monica was a sunny loft with an ocean view or a decaying dungeon that smelled like cat pee. It ended up being somewhere in between. It didn't smell like pee, but let's just say the place had a ton of potential. At least it was free, spacious-ish, and sixteen blocks from the beach. I wasn't complaining. I will say that moving into the home of a single, forty-something hoarder for three months right as you're emerging from a bad breakup can be a little tricky. You spend a lot of time lying on her quilted bed, watching her Persian cats claw at stacks of withered crafting magazines, and praying you'll fall in love again and not die alone, single, and surrounded by stuff. So. Much. Stuff.

If that story didn't renew your faith in the universe, I can't say I blame you, but check this out. March 2010 is when I got the pink slip at my job. For the next few months, I looked for work and took random jobs blogging for a lamp store and babysitting. As you can imagine, I wasn't feeling especially fancy during that time. Then, lo and behold, a professor from grad school emailed me, like a big-hearted celestial bodyguard: WE'LL BE AT THE CABIN FROM JULY 2 TO JULY 23 IF YOU WANT TO STAY AT THE HOUSE.

"Yes!" I'd been to this house. There was no clutter. My professor and her wife were in a loving relationship. There was a deck and a garden full of flowers and a freezer and an oven and a kitchen that was approximately the size of eight and a half porta-potties. She gave me the tour, told me when to water the lemon tree and how to work the thermostat (the thermostat!), and handed me the key, which was decorated in a colorful peacock-feather pattern. All thoughts of lamp blogging were swiftly deleted from my mind.

During those blissful weeks in July, I'd linger in the frozen section of the grocery store, leisurely picking the perfect flavor of ice cream, since I had a temporary freezer to store it in. I usually splurged and went with flavors like Peach Saffron or Cabernet Fig Rosemary. Pretentious, I know, but I was living the high life. And remember that Brokenomics is about knowing when to save and when to splurge. And that $5 ice cream was delicious and made me feel like Reese Witherspoon when she wasn't taking out the trash. It also didn't max out my credit cards.

The beauty of house-sitting is that you can pay rent on a tiny apartment *and* have a garden, a Jacuzzi, an outdoor shower, and a king-sized bed, at least for a time. The trick is to not get attached, like Buddha says. Don't get attached to their sectional sofa or their herb garden. Don't fall in love with their massive DVD collection or their double-headed shower that's bigger than your closet. While we're on the subject, here are a few more "dos and don'ts" from a house-sitting expert. That's me. I'm the expert.

Do: Clean, water the plants, conserve electricity, respect their privacy, throw out rotten food, wash the sheets and towels before you leave, take out the trash, leave everything exactly like it was when you arrived. And leave a thank-you note. That's classy.

Don't: Play beer pong on their reclaimed-wood cocktail table; kill, starve, or otherwise neglect anything that's living in the house other than roaches; or go through their drawers and cabinets (you wouldn't want someone doing that to you—and, seriously, you don't want to find things like giant dildos or DVDs with titles like *Anal Andy*). You also shouldn't make a mess, break their African masks, or refuse to leave.

The last one is important. Usually, when a house-sitting gig comes to an end, I'm pretty excited to squeeze back into my beach bungalow with my own utilitarian bed and my own micro closet. Sometimes, though, I want to cry and chain myself to the freezer door because the thought of parting with my Saffron Fig Cabernet sorbet is just too devastating. It's at times like those when you must remember Buddha. Don't get attached. Do not covet thy acquaintance's house, no matter how badly you want to become one with their Sleep Number bed and their zillion-thread-count sheets.

You can go home again, and you must, or they might get a restraining order.

IV.

TRAVEL AND LEISURE

Broad, wholesome, charitable views of men and things cannot be acquired by vegetating in one little corner of the earth all one's lifetime.
—Mark Twain[8]

I saw the world. I learnt of new cultures. I flew across an ocean. I wore women's clothing. Made a friend. Fell in love. Who cares if I lost a wager?
—Jules Verne, *Around the World in 80 Days*

---

8. Twain, Mark. *The Innocents Abroad* 1869, American Publishing Company

22

PLANES, TRAINS, AND ACUTE NERVOUS BREAKDOWNS

Ah, first class. The ease of being whisked to the airport or rooftop heliport by your trusty driver. The elegant roll of your Louis Vuitton valise as it passes ratty backpacks and broken Walmart suitcases hobbling pitifully on one wheel. Sure, the security line may seem a bit pesky and dirty, but when you remind yourself that our national security depends on it, it feels like less of a nuisance.

Once through, you arrive at the gate just as they pre-pre-board your class. First class. Elite first class. Before the babies and small children and elderly wheelchair-bound passengers with oxygen tanks are allowed on, there you are, easing back into a plush seat while a smiling flight attendant bestows upon you a warm, moist towel, homemade vegan cookies, and a glass—not a plastic cup like the peons in coach get—a glass of fine champagne. Sit back, relax, and enjoy the flight indeed!

Is this what traveling first class is like? Who the hell knows—not me. I'm guessing your version of plane travel, like mine, goes something like this: "That package of six peanuts will cost $10 and your flight is severely delayed and we can't do a thing about that screaming child behind you kicking your seat like a Muay Thai boxer and our in-flight movie would have been a nice distraction for you but the system's broken. Have a nice flight, asshole."

For most of us, traveling means bumping our heads on the overhead compartment as we take our seats (even if we're 5'2") and deciding between a $15 lettuce-and-mayo sandwich or a $14 roll stuffed with something that you assume is supposed to be turkey. Or maybe it's bologna. No, that's ham. Is it some sort of salami? In this situation, it's best not to overanalyze the cold cuts. The wiser option is to bring your own food on the plane or starve until you reach your destination.

First class versus coach might seem unfair, but if you're on a plane or a boat or a train, you're traveling somewhere, and that's pretty nice. Traveling doesn't have to equal trekking around the globe with servants in tow or flying to Tahiti on a whim. Some people like to stay at quaint bed-and-breakfasts in Morocco, and others are content to plunk themselves poolside at the Flagstaff La Quinta for some much needed R & R. Some grown adults get amped about their yearly jaunt to Disneyland to spin in a cup at the Mad Tea Party and take photos with Goofy. I would say that kind of trip is a tragic waste of money if you don't have kids. It's also a tragic waste of money if you do have kids, which is why early on I recommended raising a potted plant instead of a human infant. But it's your life to live, and your bank account to cry over when you get home and realize you blew three hundred bucks on Mickey Mouse merchandise.

Travel—especially plane travel—can be stressful. They charge for bags, they take away your favorite shower gel because it's one ounce over the limit, and they can see your underwear when they body scan you. Some have said that was just the early models, but unless they created a laser that puts black bars over our undergarments in the X-ray, I'm not buying it. If you don't want to check a bag, but you need to bring a purse and two bags onboard, here's a little Jason Bourne/Evelyn Salt-esque trick I devised: stuff your purse into one of the bags, then try and cram both of those into the bigger bag, and try to stand up straight and look normal as you walk past the ticket agent. Also, if you're getting frustrated and feel your blood pressure spiking due to a delay or a cancellation or lost luggage, don't yell at the overworked and underpaid airport employees. At least you're going somewhere. They have to stand there and deal with jerks like you. So don't be a jerk. Unless they're being jerks. Then you can retaliate by asking for a manager.

In addition to not acting like an asshole, I've learned two incredibly important travel lessons along the way, and I'd like to share them with you now. These lessons came out of an experience I had traveling by foot rather than by planes or trains or yachts, but they apply to any sort of travel. Even teleporting.

A few years ago, I experienced my first New York City winter. One blizzard-riddled day as I was hurrying through the streets to run an errand for my unpaid internship, I slipped on the sidewalk, landed on my tailbone, bit my lip, stood up, and hobbled into the closest store which, this being Chelsea, was a men's clothing boutique. The two guys working there seemed to care more about the snow I tracked in than they did about the twisted I'm-in-excruciating-pain-please-pity-me look on my face. Looking at them staring at me in disgust, I suddenly understood how gnats must feel every day of their miserable little lives. After a few moments of silence, during which time the thought, "Fucking New Yorkers!" spun round and round in my head several times, I headed back into the whipping wind and snow.

Once outside, I careened down the sidewalk and struggled with my umbrella, which I desperately needed to open since the snow was slushy and when it hit my face it felt like tiny daggers rather than soft puffy snowflakes. The devilish wind ricocheted off the street and torpedoed upward, slamming into my sad and wimpy $5 umbrella and flipping it inside out like a bowl. Feeling my temper start to rise, I let my aggression out by cramming the broken umbrella into a trashcan with brute force. Exposed to the elements, my hair was stuck to my face and nearly blinding me. But then, like a mirage, *she* appeared.

She had on a fancy, shiny raincoat. Her dark hair was perfectly in place, as if it were immune to the evil blizzard, and her shiny boots seemed to glide through the snow. Her umbrella remained perfectly perched above her perfectly dry head. We walked toward each other. Who the hell was this person with the magical raincoat? Why wasn't her umbrella turning inside out and sideways too? Bitch! Then, just as we passed each other, I realized why: I'd just witnessed Anne Hathaway, gliding down the street in a Manhattan blizzard, like Glenda the Good Witch descending in her perfect pink bubble. I'm not too into psychic phenomena, but I swear she had some sort of magical movie star bubble around her. Or maybe her umbrella was Prada or something. Whatever the reason, it happened, and it taught me two very important lessons:

- Budget travel is stressful, even on foot. Learn to take it in stride.

- No matter what *Us Weekly* says, stars are *not* just like us. They travel in magical protective bubbles courtesy of Prada.

23

COUCH POTATO TODAY,
GONE TOMORROW

Couch-surfing gets a bad rap. There's the negative kind of couch-surfing, where you're more like a couch potato than a couch-surfer and you're mooching off your friends and letting life pass you by as you play *Assassin's Creed IV: Black Flag* and eat Ding Dongs for dinner using a Frisbee as a plate. Then there's the positive kind, where you have a plan in place and you've made a conscious decision to save some money by sleeping on a couch for a finite amount of time so you can go travel or pay off a debt. We'll be focusing on the latter kind.

One day, during my post-college kleptomania phase, when I was dating guys whose job description could most accurately be described as "unemployed painter with delusions of grandeur," I had an epiphany. It's not as if the heavens opened and some pink-cheeked cherubs flew down to the dirty stoop I was moping on to whisper in my ear, but the moment felt holy enough for me to rise from the stoop as techno blared from the shoe store across the street and proclaim: "I have got to get the fuck out of here."

I'd spent months wondering what I was supposed to do with my life and who I was and all those other existential questions you only have the luxury of asking when you're young, single, narcissistic, and free. In that instant, I knew: I needed to leave Los Angeles and the stoop and my pay-nothing job and the love interests who enjoyed ashing their cigarettes into the pockets of their torn flannel shirts. I really knew how to pick 'em back then, as they say. I needed to go see the world and get my head straight. And so I did. Not to sound corny, but it was one of the best things I've ever done, and it did change my life. Again, not in an earth-shattering, divine-intervention kind of way, but in little ways—the ones that are more mundane than cosmological. Humdrum revelations can be just as life changing as divine flashes of insight.

Obviously, for most of us, taking off to travel on a whim can be a financial risk. Whether you're just out of college and facing a pile of debt or you're in your twenties or thirties or forties and contemplating a career change, buying a plane ticket and seeing the world might bring one or more of the following words to mind:

- Impossible
- Stupid
- Luxurious
- Expensive
- Irresponsible
- Puerile
- Deranged

If you're working at a diner during the day and using your philosophy degree as a dartboard to pass the time at night, a trip to Europe or Asia or South America might seem impossible, stupid, and irresponsible. Only you know what's right for you and what your bank statement says, but I can tell you how I made it work at a time when I was living off a steady diet of popcorn, Shake 'N Bake potatoes, and mustard. I felt literally bankrupt, and my soul felt bankrupt too. If you think that sounds melodramatic, you try emerging from a fog where you realize that your life is a mess and the jerks you've been dating aren't very nice and their bands suck too. "Bankrupt" is a pretty apt description of how that feels. Also, "stupid."

So, once you've decided to travel, the next big question is: where to go? Life isn't a movie, so I didn't close my eyes, spin a globe, and point to determine where in the world I'd wind up. I knew exactly where I wanted to go: Europe. Pretty original, right? I'd never been to Europe, and I was in the midst of an all-consuming Henry Miller phase. All I read was Henry Miller and Anaïs Nin. They drank wine in Paris cafés. They made love in French boudoirs. They ate baguettes. They quoted Baudelaire and Rimbaud! And Henry Miller couch-surfed too.

The next question to ask when contemplating a trip: how in the hell do I pay for this? Here's how I did it:

1. Bought a plane ticket
2. Got a waitressing job
3. Quit my pay-nothing cubicle job
4. Got a second waitressing job
5. Got a third waitressing job
6. Moved out of my apartment and moved onto my friend's couch for three months

That all sounds about as glamorous as moving into your truck for five years, but it worked. Before you run out and do the six things listed above without a second thought, which I'm sure you were about to do because my word is that powerful, let me break them down.

First, buying the ticket. You can't really go far away if you don't buy the ticket, so obviously this is a major step. If you just think about buying the ticket and talk about it constantly without ever clicking PURCHASE, years will go by and then you'll be on your deathbed babbling to your soul (which is hovering above your body, FYI) and saying, "Why didn't I buy that ticket to Estonia!?" And then you're dead.

Now, if buying a ticket to travel will jeopardize your family or your finances or put you in any danger of going broke or defaulting on your loans—please don't buy it. It's tricky because on the one hand, you cannot overthink this too much, but on the other hand you need to be responsible. Maybe you should work for a year and save up *before* buying a ticket to Greenland. I met several people traveling in Europe who would work at a hostel or a rafting company or a restaurant for a while and save money for the next leg of their trip. Obviously that would require that you travel for an extended period and that kind of trip takes not just money but the ability to tolerate living out of a backpack, washing your ugly utilitarian clothes only sporadically, and—when the going gets rough—sleeping in a dorm-style room with several strangers who smell like stale cheese, beer, dirt, and cigarettes. It sounds rough, but it can be life-affirming, I swear. You should buy a ticket if you can and if you feel the need, but please have some sort of plan. I had a job to go back to in Los Angeles, so that gave me some comfort, knowing I wouldn't go home completely destitute and adrift.

Next, I got a job serving greasy breakfasts to surfers and junkies and character actors near the beach. It was a dive, but the money was shockingly good. Probably because everyone who ate there was drunk and had no clue what they were tipping. It was the kind of place where you find a lot of minibar bottles of whiskey on the ground after your shift because your clientele likes to secretly spike their morning coffee. The place was a block from the beach, and one morning a woman finished eating breakfast only to discover that a whole seagull feather was hidden underneath her Denver omelet. That wasn't even the worst part. The worst part is that when I apologized profusely, as if I'd placed the feather there as an act of server sabotage, the woman looked at me blankly and said, "It doesn't matter." And then she popped a home fry in her mouth. She wasn't bothered at all. I'm sure her DIY Irish coffee helped.

I got used to this sort of thing after a while. This was when raves were big, and it was pretty normal to see people twirl into the restaurant at seven o'clock in the morning still high from candy-flipping or whatever they were on. They'd usually order pancakes with beatific smiles on their faces, and then, instead of eating them, they'd knead the pancakes with their bare hands until they formed what they thought looked like a yin-yang or a pile of dough that resembled a wolf howling at a moon. These customers were incredibly generous tippers, as you can imagine. That went a long way toward making their dayglo wigs and candy pacifiers tolerable.

On one particularly glorious day at the dive, I walked into the dingy kitchen and saw the chef drop a half-cooked veggie patty onto the scuzzy floor and quickly scoop it back into the skillet. You're never supposed to mess with the chef but instinct took over and I blurted, "No." She glared at me for a few seconds but then threw it out because, come on. That's just gross. Anyway, I made money there, despite the fact that it was a cesspool of culinary nightmares. The place was a neighborhood institution when I worked there, which should tell you all you need to know about Venice, California, at that time. It closed down a few years ago and is now a fancy "farm-to-table" restaurant, which should tell you all you need to know about Venice, California and gentrification and food trends in the twenty-first century.

Now that you've lost your appetite, let's move on to the "quit my job" part of the plan. As a rule, you shouldn't quit a job unless you have another one lined up—unless you've worked your ass off and have made enough to take a much-deserved break. Once I got the job at Seagull Feather Heaven, I quit my nine-to-five cubicle gig and got two more server jobs. That might sound extreme, but it wasn't too bad. Of course, you don't have to wait tables to save up travel money, but it does pay pretty well (at least in America), and it's an easier job to quit than being a CEO or a neurosurgeon. You have to pay for your own health insurance though, so there's that.

And now, the final step: couch-surfing. First, you must have very generous friends who own a decent-sized couch. Next, they have to really like you. Occupying a living room isn't the height of glamour, but I saved over $1,500 by doing just that for three months before I took off on my twelve-week trip to Europe. I paid my friends $200 a month, made them dinners, and stayed clean and quiet. Except when we had late-night dance parties. The biggest sacrifice was sharing the couch and the living room with a beast called Hepcat (R.I.P.). I love all animals, except maybe hyenas and ferrets, and Hepcat was much better than either of those. Still, she had her issues. Anyone who ever met her understands. Everyone else probably thinks I'm a cat terrorist. It's not true. I love cats. I even loved Hepcat, even though she was possessed by the devil. That's not an exaggeration. If you'd met her, you'd know.

Regardless, if you can make it happen, traveling and seeing the world is worth a little couch-surfing and table-waiting. It widens your perspective, helps you realize that the world doesn't revolve around you, teaches you resilience and patience and street smarts, and helps you figure things out so you can stop moping on the stoop and serving seagull feathers to drunk strangers. Traveling is more expensive now, so maybe the days of budget backpacking are over, which is too bad. But if you really want to do it, there are always tables to wait and couches to sleep on and places to go.

Do it while you can, because eventually you'll get older and your tolerance for hostels and backpacks will plummet as precipitously as your fertility, and traveling will involve actual hotels and rolling suitcases. I've graduated to the hell-no-will-I-ever-stay-in-a-hostel-again stage of life, but it was a lot of fun while it lasted.

24

SOMEBODY KNOWS SOMEBODY
WHO LIVES IN PARIS

N ow it's time to talk about one of the most important rules of budget travel: go where you know someone. I'm not saying you should use people, obviously, but if you're dying to go to Paris and you have a friend who is living alone in a three-bedroom condo in Singapore—go to Singapore. If Celeste, your second cousin twice removed, is playing volleyball in Lithuania, why not check that place out? Lithuania is fun. Probably.

However, you should proceed with caution when it comes to the "go where you know someone rule" if one or more of these statements applies:

- They hate you
- You hate them
- You slept together and you never bothered texting/calling/acknowledging their existence afterward
- They have a newborn
- You have a newborn that you're bringing with you

- They still believe *Crash* deserved to win the Oscar for Best Picture[9]
- They live in a teepee
- You're bringing fifteen suitcases, teepee or bust
- They're a klepto
- They smack their breakfast cereal
- Kevin Federline is their favorite rapper
- You plan to ask them for a loan
- They owe you $25,000
- They tried to drown you in first grade
- There's a warrant out for their arrest

Other than that, it's a totally viable option.

---

9. Brokeback Mountain deserved to win, goddamnit.

25

WEDDING SEASON:
THEIR DREAM, YOUR NIGHTMARE

Ladies,

Some of the bridesmaid dresses are now on sale. If you have yet to purchase, it's probably best to do so ASAP! Please hurry and do not forget. And make sure you buy silver heels too if you don't have any. Small jewelry is best, no big bangles please! If you haven't told me whether you want your hair and makeup done let me know ASAP. It's $150 for each. Can't wait!

xoxo

As far as pre-wedding emails from a bride-to-be go, that one is pretty tame. I feel extremely lucky that none of my friends has morphed into a Bridezilla leading up to her big day. Scratch that. There was that one time that my friend Courtney lost her mind ten minutes before the ceremony and screamed, "My bridesmaids are all bitches!" Was she offended by the way we were holding our bouquets as we stood in a single-file line wearing unflattering $300 dresses and uncomfortable metallic heels in her honor? Sometimes people freak out in the months and weeks leading up to the happiest day of their lives. If you're in the wedding, it's your job to bite your tongue and help them get past the "I do" part so they can go back to being a nice, normal, sane human being.

Weddings are pricey for the people throwing them, of course, unless they're eloping and stopping for pierogies after. They're also expensive for the legions of us who are asked to be in the wedding—the esteemed bridesmaids and groomsmen who feel honored to stand by our friends on their big day, but who also feel secretly stressed out about the tuxes and dresses and parties and gifts and plane tickets and hotels and mental abuse that lies ahead.

Once you reach a certain age, a barrage of delicate, embossed wedding invitations start flying at you like daggers. Once this begins, get ready for a series of events that will test both your survival instincts and your threshold for pain. You love your friends and want to support them but, when it comes to weddings, that support isn't just emotional—it's financial. What can you do when someone you love and care about asks you to plan their bachelor or bachelorette party and fly to another country to watch them walk down the aisle? You suck it up and say yes is what you do.

> **What can you do when someone you love and care about asks you to plan their bachelor or bachelorette party and fly to another country to watch them walk down the aisle? You suck it up and say "yes" is what you do.**

You break into a cold sweat and start planning. And, most important, you vow that one day, you'll exact your revenge by making them fly first class to Tasmania and wear Armani outfits when it's your turn to get hitched.

I've planned bachelorette parties in Los Angeles, New Orleans, Palm Springs, Austin, and Guerneville. Are you impressed yet? I'm talking burlesque shows, hotel pools that have people walking around handing out free popsicles, fun dinners, and games where you make penises out of Play-Doh. Planning a bachelorette or bachelor party on a budget does not mean you will wind up sitting in a tent with the bride or groom and the rest of the bridesmaids or groomsmen, eating yeast, drinking Boone's Farm Strawberry

Hill, and wearing hand-me-down penis hats. You just have to plan ahead, and you have to be honest and communicate with everyone about the cost, which is usually easier said than done.

As an example, let's look at the most recent bachelorette party I helped plan. It was for Allie, one of my closest college friends who was and is a surgeon. I'm not telling you this so you can marvel at how successful and intelligent my friends are. I'm telling you this so you understand that half of the people paying for the bachelorette party were doctors, and the other half consisted of: a freelance writer (me!), a massage therapist, a teacher, and a therapist therapist. We all knew each other at least a little bit, but talking about money with another human being is always awkward and embarrassing, no matter how close you are. Lauren, one of the doctors, was the maid of honor, and for whatever reason I became the intermediary between the two factions. We weren't at war, but when money enters the picture it can sometimes feel that way, even if, under normal circumstances, you genuinely like the other people involved.

We knew the date of the bachelorette party, and we knew we were going to Palm Springs, but, up until four weeks before the big weekend, that's about all we knew. And so, panic set in. Kate, my massage therapist friend, needed to know how much this would be costing, and so did I. Would we be staying in a luxury suite or sharing normal rooms with pullout couches? Were we dining at Michelin-starred restaurants or eating at pizza joints? Since a doctor was in charge, we assumed the worst. At least plane fare wasn't part of the equation. Our texts got a little hysterical.

Kate: *Have you heard from Lauren? Where are we staying?!!*
DG: *No idea—we need to know!*
Kate: *I know! WTF. Will you ask her?*
DG: *Ugh. OK. I hate this. HATE IT!*

I put on my big girl pants and texted the maid of honor. I'd like you to note the smiley face in the following exchange, because it's the ultimate twenty-first-century symbol of passive-aggressive bullshit behavior.

> **DG:** *Hey Lauren! Do you know where we're staying yet? Just trying to figure out budget :)*
>
> **Lauren:** *In Bali!*

"What the fuck?!" I said out loud, to my phone. More hysterical texting with Kate ensued.

> **DG:** *I asked where we're staying and she said "in Bali!" That's not funny*
>
> **Kate:** *WTF we need to know!*
>
> **DG:** *I know! This is so awkward*
>
> **Kate:** *What do we do? The rooms might end up being $500 and I won't be able to go. Allie will kill me*

Kate's texts set my imagination ablaze. I had visions of us sipping Dom Pérignon and cackling as we gorged on Maine lobsters. We went back and forth playing the martyrs and getting creative with emoticon combinations to let out our frustration, like pairing a crying face with the stack of money that has wings attached to it, or the gun with the slot machine. The emoji of the girl getting the head massage is a perennial favorite of mine. It captures just how I'm feeling when stressed: soulless, two-dimensional, and desperately in need of a temple rub.

A few days after the Bali text, I got an email from Lauren. Turns out she actually was in Bali when she texted, so the joke was on me I guess. When I wrote back, I didn't use any smiley faces or emojis. I explained to Lauren that some of us were on a budget and needed to start planning for the weekend, and, wouldn't you know, she didn't blackball me or call me a penniless nuisance. She totally understood. Turns out doctors need to budget too, or at least they remember what it's like. We got on the phone and had an honest and productive talk about feathered boas and hotel rooms, and just when we were settled on a budget and a plan, I blurted, "We should have a lingerie shower too!" Curse my stupid Southern roots.

If you don't know, a lingerie shower is a bachelorette party "must" where I'm from. Sometime during the weekend, usually before dinner on the first night, you sit around sipping cocktails out of penis straws and everyone gives the bride-to-be some sort of lingerie gift. It can be sexy and pretty, or it can be a "slutty cheerleader outfit" and some anal beads. It's best to do it in a public place like a hotel lobby or a bar, for maximum mortification. The point is, it's an extra cost and I don't know why I suggested it. Well, I do know. When you love your friends, you want to do nice things for them for their bachelorette or bachelor party, even if it costs extra.

Lauren agreed to the lingerie shower but then added, "I'm so afraid to ask people to spend money. Would you mind telling everyone so people can plan?" Fair enough. I crafted a beautiful email extolling the virtues of the lingerie shower, explaining how much fun it would be. "You can get her a teddy or you can get something funny like a Door Jam Sex Sling and really embarrass her!!" There were a few smiley faces in that email, as you can imagine. In the end, everyone was more than happy to do it, even Kate. Or at least they pretended to be happy and then sent each other pissed-off, hysterical texts behind my back. I'll never know.

Once we'd agreed on a hotel and a food budget that worked for everyone, spending the money on our friend was a pleasure instead of a burden. Just remember that when wedding season starts taking over your life, you need to plan ahead, communicate, grin and bear it, and never, ever let the bride or groom see you stress about money. You can do that in secret, using as many emoji as you need. Once you've agreed on the plan and you're all together for the night or weekend, you better jump in and have fun. Or, if you really can't afford to fly to the Bahamas for your friend's nuptials, don't beat yourself up or go into debt over it. If she's a true friends, she'll understand.

After all the stress of planning, Allie's bachelorette party was drama-free. We swam, drank, danced, and had the lingerie shower that I'm sure made my ancestors proud. There was only one minor altercation. It happened in a crowded club on the second night, when I noticed that Allie wasn't wearing the tiara we'd gotten her. It was the kind that said BACHELORETTE in glittery letters and had a little tuft of pink tulle poking out of it. I scanned the dance floor like a ninja until I saw it perched on the head of a stranger gyrating to Rihanna. I marched across the club like a courageous Viking outfitted in a floral-patterned romper to reclaim what was rightly ours. I'd become a ninja *and* a Viking, which can happen when you drink a few martinis.

"Excuse me, but that's my friend's tiara," I said to the drunk klepto. "WHAT?!" she yelled, spilling her drink a little as she straightened the tiara on her head.

I screamed over the music, "You're wearing my friend's tiara and it's her bachelorette party!" I then pointed at Allie. She was dancing and laughing and couldn't care less about the stolen tiara. I was still determined to save the day and get those fake diamonds back, though, because that's what bridesmaids are for. I braced for a showdown, even though I'd never been in a fistfight and would crawl across the dance floor on my hands and knees like a toddler if this stranger tried to hit me. She didn't try to hit me, though. She just pulled the tiara off of her head and handed it back, dancing all the while. I accepted it with grace and integrity, as a warrior should.

I returned to my clan triumphant and handed Allie her crown. No one made a big deal about it, but I felt like someone should have handed me a Bridesmaid of the Year award or a goblet of mead. The plastic tiara only cost about seven bucks, but we did pay for the thing. It wasn't about the money though. It was Allie's night, and that was her tiara. We were just there to make sure she got the most out of it.

HOW TO FIX YOUR CAR WITH VELCRO (AND OTHER TRICKS NO MECHANIC WILL TELL YOU)

"What is the problem with your car?" the mechanic asked.

"I don't know," I said, shaking my head and cradling the driver's side mirror in my arms. We were standing in a dingy alley because this was the kind of body shop that existed in secret, in a hidden alleyway with no sign.

"Why does this keep happening to you?" he marveled.

"I don't know," I repeated, extending the decapitated car part to him like a sacrificial offering. I didn't want to think about what it all meant. I was in no mood to ponder what the universe was trying to tell me by having a stranger knock the driver's side mirror off my car for the second time in four months, without leaving a note. I just needed this guy to stick the mirror back on. Hopefully at a discounted rate.

Even though I was in no mood for hysterical philosophizing, I did have an hour to kill while he tried to reattach the mirror, so I started asking myself the big questions. What did it all mean? Did I have an enemy stalker following me around Los Angeles, lying in wait until I parked so they could whack my side mirror with a baseball bat? What message was this psycho trying to send? Or was it the universe trying to teach me a lesson? Was the mirror a sign? Was this a lesson in auto mechanics, or vanity? Or were people in Los Angeles just a bunch of shitheads who don't leave notes when they swipe your car and send your side mirror flying into the bushes?

I'm not so vain that the universe would need to sit me down and teach me a lesson about egomania. When I make love to my reflection, it usually happens in the rearview mirror, not the side mirror. And so, after a four-second soul search, I came to the conclusion that this was happening because people are shitheads. It was the only plausible explanation. Feeling pleased with my powers of deductive reasoning, I pulled out my compact and applied some lipstick as I sat on a crate in the empty alleyway, waiting.

Because my car and I have been through so many ups and downs (bird poop, peeling paint, flat tires, overheating, funny froglike sounds coming from under the hood, now the double mirror bashing), I know a lot about auto mechanic stuff. OK, maybe not a lot. I can't replace a transmission or clean the catalytic converter, but when your car has as much "personality" as mine does, you learn a few tricks. You learn what a catalytic converter does, that ignition coils exist, and that there is such a thing as a water pump and that the cap for the pump costs extra. If you want to know how to get the most out of your car and not get ripped off, stick around because I've been around the block a few times. Slowly. With a sputtering engine and some pretty squeaky brakes.

Before we move forward, there's one caveat: if your car is a McLaren or a Bentley, I cannot help you (but please keep reading). If you're happy with a car that runs well, gets you from place to place, and looks presentable, then let's do this. Much like when I encounter mansions with rolling, green, rainbow-speckled lawns, when I see a very expensive, shiny convertible sports car, my first thought is, "What about pigeons, or drunk teenagers?" There's something nice about not having to worry about all that. If your

Bentley gets scratched, you are going to fly into a tizzy as if a meteorite had just struck it. Don't get me wrong, a Ferrari Dino is one of the hottest things on the planet, and I love looking at them. I've never actually seen one in person, but if staring at Google image searches counts, I'm pretty much an expert. I'd love to ride around in one, but if I owned a Dino, I'd waste way too much time worrying about it getting stolen or nicked or used as a seagull commode. I'd rather just Google them every once in a while and let someone else's blood pressure spike when the beautiful car gets keyed. That's just how I roll. Like a baller.

In case you're on the edge of your seat waiting to hear what happened with my car and the back-alley auto mechanic, he did reattach my side mirror that day. It can't be adjusted anymore, but I'm the only one who drives the thing so who cares. It's in better shape than it was when I inherited it from my sister. At that time the casing was cracked and it had silver duct tape wrapped around the wound like a futuristic Band-Aid—if the future was a cheesy, low-budget 1970s science-fiction movie. I tore the duct tape off one day in a fit of pride. Duct tape on the outside of your car is embarrassing and should be avoided at all costs, unless you have an "art car" and duct tape is part of the aesthetic. If that's the case—good luck going on dates.

No matter what kind of car you have, I strongly suggest that you start an "I Didn't See This Shit Coming Fund" (IDSTSCF) by putting away $10 from every paycheck or socking away $500 to the cause the second you buy a car. If you were wise enough to take an auto mechanics class somewhere along the way and can fix cars yourself, your fund can be smaller than the one the rest of us bozos need. It's never fun when your day starts out perfectly grand—you're driving down the road, happy as can be—and then you hear a hissing sound quickly followed by white smoke wafting from the hood. This is why you need the fund. It's so you can be somewhat calm when the mechanic tells you it'll cost two grand to fix the problem. Instead of screaming at him, you can become an internally angry sociopath and use your inside voice when you say, in your brain, "Motherf&^76 bull&*^& this is a damn *&# situation! But, at least I have the fund . . ."

In addition to the IDSTSCF, there are some fabulous fix-it tricks that might help you save money when it comes to your car's maintenance. Some might call them "ghetto" fix-it tricks, but I prefer the term "fabulous."

DIY. Do you pull into a body shop every time a headlight or taillight goes out or your wiper blades need to be replaced? How much do they charge you? Probably a lot more than the pack of $6 lights you can get at the auto-supply store. Replacing headlights and taillights and wiper blades are the easiest car fixes, and trust me: if I can do it, you can too. Here's another tip: if you have that green rusty buildup on your car battery, you can use Coke, lemon juice, sparkling water, or, if you're feeling decadent, some cheap champagne to clean it off. You'll not only save money, you'll also feel like a real badass. You can even wear overalls and work boots to really amp up the illusion. If you really want to get into it, go nuts and smear some charcoal on your face to make it look like car grease.

Velcro. If your engine falls out, you might not want to try and reattach it with Velcro, but you can use Velcro for small interior fixes until you have enough time and money to get them actually fixed. When the lid on the center console in my car (how's that for technical car speak?) decided that it wanted to slam up and down instead of closing, I went to the drug store, bought some Velcro, cut it into little pieces, and made a makeshift fastener. Brilliant, right? I could have paid to have someone fix it for real, but I was too resourceful (or stubborn and lazy—whichever). In a pinch, Velcro is your friend. Just not when it comes to engines, batteries, tires, carburetors . . . or anything major, really.

Upkeep. This one might seem obvious, but you'll save money in the long run if you regularly get your car serviced, including getting the oil changed and the tires checked. You can also whisper sweet nothings under the hood to keep your car's confidence up, but make sure you do it when no one is looking. (Note: you won't get that last tip in any auto mechanics class!)

Haggle. This is yet another instance when haggling is a necessary life skill. If a mechanic tells you that the ignition coil needs replacing and that it'll cost seven hundred bucks, you better start Googling the cost of ignition coils. You'll find a lot of good info via that wondrous thing called the Internet, so do your research, both on the car parts and customer reviews on the body shop itself. And never, ever blindly agree to anything a mechanic says. If the mechanic is a blood relative, like a parent—don't trust them. Even if your mechanic is your mother, the woman who gave birth to you and kept you alive while you cried and slobbered and spit up all over her, don't believe a word she says about your car. Do your research, call around, and haggle until you get them down to a price that's reasonable. (Feel free to review chapter 6 as needed.)

Threaten. If the haggling isn't going so well and you feel like you're getting ripped off, it's time to get serious. It's time for threats. I'm not saying you need to challenge them to a duel, but you do need to pull out the "Well, I'll just call customer service" card or, if you're really desperate, the dreaded, "Well, I'll just go on Yelp" trick. Yelp.com reviews are so lame. They're written by emotionally unstable crybabies who sit around in Star Wars pajamas eating Count Chocula out of the box, frantically typing negative reviews about dentists and drug stores and the UPS delivery person. You don't have to actually write the review, but, if you're fed up, it's worth tossing it out there. And if you truly have been ripped off and you're at your wit's end, calling customer service (if they have that) can work wonders.

Marry a mechanic. Some parents want their kids to marry a nice doctor or lawyer or tech genius. If I ever have kids I'm going to push them to marry a mechanic, so they'll be spared a lot of heartbreak, at least when it comes to spending money on their car. I know I said never trust a mechanic even if they're in the family, but it wouldn't hurt to have one in your pocket, just in case. Actually, I hope to hell I won't be the kind of parent to "push" a kid into anything. They can marry a damn neurosurgeon if they want to.

27

SNEAKING INTO
SWIMMING POOLS:
A LESSON IN HUMAN RIGHTS

The summers were scorching hot where I grew up. In Fort Worth, Texas, from about May to September, car seatbelts were like branding irons, lawns looked like scarecrow stuffing no matter how much you watered them, and locusts routinely dropped dead of heat exhaustion. Swimming was our only salvation. Sitting in front of the TV with the air conditioner blasting watching *Scooby-Doo* was a close second.

We didn't have a pool, but my grandparents did and it was glorious. When we couldn't go there, we'd leap through sprinklers or belly flop around in those blue baby pools with cartoony turtles printed on the plastic. One summer day my sister and I got creative with our neighbors Marlena and Troy. We each got a big black garbage bag, took it outside, filled it with water from the hose, and then just stood there on the lawn, each of us submerged like giant waterlogged beetles with human heads. This might not be the ideal picture of suburban summertime bliss. I can't see Norman Rockwell painting this tableau, but it worked for us. At least I think it did. You know those childhood memories that seem so real but so odd that you secretly question whether or not your psyche just conjured them up to mess with you? The day we made garbage bag swimming pools is one of those memories.

Whether real or improvised, pools are wonderful things in the summertime. They're wonderful things anytime, with a few exceptions. During my last two years of college, most of my friends lived in a building that we called Ghetto Melrose Place, partly because, just like on the show, all the apartments faced a swimming pool (except this one happened to have a couch at the bottom of it), and partly because everyone who lived there was a less glamorous, less wealthy, much puffier version of Amanda, Billy, Allison, and Dr. Peter Burns.

Swimming pools symbolize many things: summer, luxury, relaxation, vacation, the good life. While some people would rather sit in the dark and watch a documentary about genocide than float in a pool, I'm not one of them. I love pools, whether they're Olympic-sized, lima bean–shaped, or just for wading. If you love them too, and if you don't have one of your own, don't worry. I bet there's a treasure trove of gorgeous public pools in your area, waiting for you to sneak in and lounge beside them. I'm not saying you should hop fences and trespass at your neighbor's pool every day, but I think hotels, motels, and apartment buildings are fair game. Any hotel managers reading this should just look the other way.

I started sneaking into pools in college. Somehow, between studying all day and eating calzones at three in the morning, I staked out every apartment building in the neighborhood that had a pool, and if I felt like swimming or sprawling out on a plastic lounge chair while reading *Hamletmachine* for drama class (1945–present), I'd just hit the buzzer, tell whoever's apartment I just rang that I forgot my keys, and they'd always buzz me right up. I might feel a little weird and loser-ish doing this now that I'm way out of school, but if you're between eighteen and twenty-four, knock yourself out.

What I do still have no problem doing is sneaking into hotel pools. I understand that if you're a paying guest, you deserve a chair and a table more than some freeloader who fixes her car with Velcro, but that's also a little classist. It's not a felony to sneak into a hotel pool. There's nothing in the constitution that says it's a crime. Therefore, it's a human right. You're not stealing anything, unless you go sneak one of their fluffy towels into your bag before you leave—which you should not do.

If you want to try sneaking into the local pool, the first rule is that you need to bring your own towel. Don't be obvious about it, though. If you walk into the lobby with a giant towel, sunscreen, and an umbrella poking out of your bag, looking guilty even underneath your big sunglasses, they'll stop you and ask what room you're in, and when you stutter, "Uhhh . . . 5678?" they'll kick you out, especially if they have only four floors. Confidence is key. With your towel and everything else you'll need for the day hidden away in your bag, waltz through the lobby as if you own it. Imagine that you're Grace Kelly or Will Smith and that you are a *movie star*. If you know where the pool is, head there immediately, without making any eye contact.

If you have no clue where the pool is, walk to the elevator or the restroom, whichever is easiest to spot. If you do this, it buys you some time to scan around for any signs pointing to the pool. Just make sure you have a destination. Don't wander around looking lost like you just time-traveled there from 1869. Just go somewhere. If all else fails, get in the elevator and ask another guest where the pool is. It's not the smoothest move, but it might work. Maybe this all sounds very complicated, but with a little practice, you can master my well-researched techniques, which have been thoroughly tested.

And if you do get caught sneaking into a hotel pool and they ask you to leave, please don't try to argue by telling them they're violating your rights. Just bow your head like a serf, say, "I'm sorry sir/ma'am, I'll never do it again," and do a walk of shame out of the lobby.

Then try the next hotel down the road.

V.

FASHION AND BEAUTY

Everything has beauty, but not everyone sees it.
—Confucious

Deep down, I'm pretty superficial.
—Ava Gardner[10]

10. Gardner, Ava. *Ava: My Story*. Bantam, 1990. Courtesy of The Ava Gardner Trust.

28

YARD SALES ARE A
GIRL'S BEST FRIEND

W ho doesn't love a diamond? They're gorgeous, luxurious, and much more sparkly than a Ross Dress for Less rhinestone. They're aloof and regal. They can make you feel like a million bucks, and sometimes they actually cost that much. I have nothing against diamonds, but with all due respect to Marilyn Monroe (and to Jule Styne and Leo Robin, who wrote the song), diamonds are not a girl's best friend. If diamonds are your best friend, you might need to see a psychologist.

I know that singing, "Yard sales are a girl's best friend!" doesn't have the same *je ne sais quoi*, but if you're looking to score some extra cash, it's kind of true. I guess if you fell on hard times and you had a giant Cartier diamond to pawn you'd make more than you would selling old shoes and half-empty bottles of perfume out of your garage, but it would be much tougher to part with that diamond than it would be to sell an old ratty yoga mat. It's truly amazing to behold what people will buy from you at a yard sale: ancient flip phones, bent forks, scrunchies, a can of baked beans. I bet if you put out a pair of old socks with your name monogrammed across the toes, someone would buy them.

Besides being a great way to observe human behavior at its most bizarre (if you've seen the 7:00 AM crowd at a garage sale you know what I'm talking about), having regular yard sales might just make you richer. I'm not saying you'll get rich, but you might become a few hundred dollars rich*er*. I have a yard sale about once a year. It's the most fun way to make a buck. You clean out your closets and drawers and cabinets, throw all the stuff you're sick of on the lawn, put on some music, and watch your pocket balloon as you stuff it with cash. It's most likely a bunch of ones and quarters, but it adds up. It's like being handed free money—*and* you get rid of stuff you're not using. Getting diamonds made Marilyn Monroe want to sing. Getting dollars and quarters at a yard sale makes me want to belt out an aria.

I love having yard sales so much that I'm a little terrified of becoming one of those women who wear halter tops when they're sixty-five years old. The ones who spend their weekends throwing all the same crap on their lawn and sticking a SALE sign in the grass just because they have nothing better to do. Or maybe the weekly sales are part of their retirement plan. These people exist all over my neighborhood. Every weekend, year-round, there they are: sprawled on a plastic lounge chair, wearing their halter top and some sweatpants, drinking a Mai Tai, and haggling with customers over the price of their daughter's 'N Sync bobblehead collection or their Moody Blues 8-track tapes. I pray that's not a vision of my future, but that doesn't stop me from having yard sales and wanting to write poems about how much I love them.

There are a few things you need to know when throwing a yard sale. One is that you can also call it a garage sale or a rummage sale, and, if you're in Canada, you can call it a jumble sale. The choice is yours. Put up plenty of signs, and put an ad on Craigslist. Don't just expect people to come because your stuff is so incredible they can hear it calling to them from across town. You should also be fair with prices. If you bought a dress for $300 and you're trying to sell it for $200 even though it's hanging from a shrub in your yard, you need to lower that price way down. Or you can take it to a consignment shop. But you need to price things low. Don't get uppity about your old, used crap, no matter how amazing it once was. Trust me, no one at your garage sale cares about BCBG versus Target. OK, maybe a few people do. If you can spot them, it's OK to add a few bucks to the price. Which reminds me—don't put price tags on things. Part of the fun is being spontaneous and on your toes and pricing things on the fly. It infuses the experience with a little drama. Just try and remember whether you told the lady in the muumuu that you're charging two or three bucks for the unopened bottle of One Direction perfume she wants to buy.[11] That's important, because when you have ten people haggling with you, handing you crumpled $10 bills and expecting you to calculate how much change you owe them, it's easy for your mind to go completely blank.

You need to keep track of what you're telling people, but you also need to be loose with the haggling. You want to get rid of all this junk, so if someone offers you fifty cents instead of two bucks for a DVD of *Sex and the City 2*, take the fifty cents. Actually, you should probably just give her that movie for free. It's also good to have bags for people so they can stuff all the crap they're buying into them, and you should start the day off with a bunch of $1 bills and tons of change. I guarantee you that the first customer of the day will hand you a twenty when she's buying a mangled Slinky for a quarter. It's better to be prepared than to be pretentious and tell her to go get change. Plus you might lose a valuable customer if you send her away. Keep her in your sight. Every penny counts. I really mean that: do not lose her. See! Garage sales make me crazy.

Other than that, just sit back with your friends, do a crossword puzzle, and watch the cash come rolling in. And while it might be tempting to go blow all the proceeds on a late-afternoon bottomless mimosa brunch right after your sale ends, because you'll be flying so high from all the currency in your pocket and the serotonin coursing through your brain, it's smarter to save the money.

---

11. An actual item I sold at a yard sale in August 2014. It's called Our Moment and it smells like a mixture of cotton candy, chocolate doughnuts, and Pine-Sol.

Brunch is so fun though. And so is serotonin. Whatever. Brokenomics is all about balance so go have brunch. You earned it.

> *You want to get rid of all this junk, so if someone offers you fifty cents instead of two bucks for a DVD of* Sex and the City 2, *take the fifty cents.*

Before that brunch, when the flow of customers has dwindled and you're still left with some sad old junk, throw it all in your trunk, drive straight to the Salvation Army or Goodwill, and donate it. And, what should you ask for when you make that donation? A receipt, so you can write it all off when tax time comes around.

After brunch, you may want to spread your crumpled up $1 bills all over the bedroom floor and stare at them as greed and gluttony wage war in your soul, making you feel just like a corrupt billionaire must feel after a big deal closes. But yard sales are about much more than money. They mean something. There's a spiritual aspect to them that I don't think many people understand. You're letting go of material possessions like Buddha says to do. You've elevated to a higher plane. You are a supreme being unburdened by earthly concerns like bobbleheads and *Sex and the City 2* DVDs.

If that theory isn't working for you, then how's this: you're a financially savvy civilian who just sold a bunch of old stuff for a profit, and Buddha had nothing to do with it. That's probably the more feasible explanation. You're a micro-entrepreneur who is a few hundred bucks richer than you were the day before, and all you had to do was sit around, make up arbitrary prices for things, and watch people hand you cash. It's capitalism at its best.

29

SHAMPOO. RINSE. SPEND A GAZILLION DOLLARS ON HAIRCUTS.

s there anything more glamorous than having a hairdresser? Someone you've been going to for years, whom you can gossip with and describe to outsiders as "my wonderful hairdresser, Brian"? In my early twenties I dreamed of being one of those people with a "Brian" to call my own, and now I am.

In fact, one day last spring, I was sitting at the salon gossiping away with my wonderful hairdresser, Brian. Only his name isn't Brian.

"If you ever write about me I want you to name me Marcel," said my wonderful hairdresser . . . Marcel.

"And here's a tip for you," Marcel went on. "Boys are stupid. You should spend all your money on your hair because guys can't tell if you have hair extensions, and one of my clients has no money but she spends everything she has on her hair, and she's going on a date with Bill Maher. He's taking her to the Playboy Mansion. So just use a credit card and spend money on your hair, and when that one gets declined, just get another one!"

I adore Marcel, but I'm not sure about that advice. I'm also not sure a date with Bill Maher at the Playboy Mansion is a dream come true or a reason to splurge on hair extensions. Personally I'd rather go traipsing through the heath with Michael Fassbender than float around in the Playboy Mansion grotto with a shirtless Bill Maher. The grotto is supposedly sad and rundown, whereas a heath seems romantic and germ-free. Another plus of traipsing through a heath on a date is that your hair can be a little wild and free—and by wild and free I mean recently highlighted and cut and flowing in the wind, but without any costly hair extensions.

Some people are so low-maintenance that they cut their own hair and don't bother coloring it, even when it's streaked with grey. If you're that person, then god bless you. You probably save a ton of money. I wish I could be like you, embracing every grey strand because you believe that it doesn't mean you're aging, it just means that you've really lived. In those silver filaments you see that time you fought off a panther in Africa or the silent retreat you endured in Nepal, while the rest of us see in our own grey streaks our inevitable descent into the abyss. I will never be like you. I won't embrace grey hair; I'll curse each and every one and call it a little asshole upon discovery, at least until I'm in my seventies. Maybe then I'll get over myself and start looking at them as badges of a life well lived. For now, they're the enemy, and I will not let them win. Maybe this is why the universe knocked the side mirror off my car more than once.

Most of us do go to a salon to get our hair done, and it's not cheap. For men it usually costs less—go figure. Some men highlight their hair and spend hundreds on cuts each month, but most guys I know pay about thirty bucks. Such is life in the twenty-first century. Much like auto mechanics, hair stylists are trained to do things that most of us simply cannot manage. Haven't you ever tried replicating the blowout you get at the salon only to look in the mirror and see a giant Phil Spector-ish bird's nest on your head? I tried highlighting my hair a few times. In middle school I had a lovely yellowish burnt orange tint thanks to the Sun-In I drenched my hair with all summer. That didn't cost much. I also tried using one of those home highlighting kits once. I think I'd rather go grey than look like that again.

While getting your hair done by a professional can be expensive, you can comfort yourself by remembering they're providing a service you probably can't do at home.

So, while getting your hair done by a professional can be expensive, you can comfort yourself by remembering they're providing a service you probably can't do at home. And let's face it—a lot of us are vain when it comes to our hair. That's why Hair Club for Men exists, and about 6,000 different products for women. When you see Tina Fey flipping around her shiny locks in those Garnier Nutrisse ads, you probably don't think, "I need to run to CVS and get some of that shampoo immediately." You probably think, "Man, I wish I could afford a celebrity hairdresser." I'm not saying that Tina Fey isn't selling the hell out of Garnier Nutrisse. I am saying that most of us are aware that your hair doesn't magically get that silky and bouncy just by putting some $5 shampoo on it. Or maybe I'm just jaded. I've never tried that shampoo.

Brokenomics is about saving money, but if adding salon visits to your budget is doable and worth it, then you should find a Marcel of your own. Find someone you trust, and negotiate a price with them right off the bat. You actually can do that, you know. If the salon's website says $150 for highlights, see if they'll do it for $100 or $125. It helps if you're extremely nice and courteous, and if you bring them cookies or wine or comic books on occasion. And tip well, obviously. Marcel gives me a generous deal because:

- He's wonderful
- We've become buddies
- I've referred half my friends to him
- I bring him cookies and comic books

Find someone you trust and who gives you a deal, and refer everyone you know to them. Professional hair care is expensive, but it doesn't have to bankrupt you.

If, on the other hand, you are maxing out credit cards like the mystery woman who went out with with Bill Maher, you need to either find a cheaper hair salon or get really good at using those home highlighting kits and cutting your hair yourself. Maybe you're lucky enough to have a friend who is a hairdresser, or maybe you're married to one—even better. If not, put it into your budget, negotiate a price, come bearing gifts, and forge a deep and meaningful relationship with your own Marcel, because unless you're fine trudging around town with a silvery typhoon on your head, paying to have someone help you look halfway decent is pretty important.

For example, who would you give a job to: the candidate with the bad dye job and a jagged bowl cut, or the candidate who looks like a Garnier Nutrisse ad? Maybe that scenario is a little extreme. It's not about looking perfect; it's about feeling confident. If the jagged bowl cut you do yourself makes you feel like a superstar and your dream job is punk singer or Etsy entrepreneur, then go for it. If not, just make sure you don't go into debt because of your salon bill. And please don't get hair extensions so you can score a date at Nobu with Jesse James. I think that's a terrible reason to spend money, though many people in Los Angeles would probably disagree.

30

WHY BUYING GREAT SHOES IS SMARTER THAN INVESTING IN THE STOCK MARKET

Unless you're a barefoot runner living off the grid in the canyons of Mexico, you probably love or at least like shoes. They're easy to fall in love with—you can eat five éclairs right before you try them on and your foot size will be the same. Plus, you can be suddenly 5'4" when you're actually 5'1". And, unlike with stocks, investing in a beautiful, durable pair of shoes won't leave you wondering where your money went. It went right there, on your feet.

The whole shoe-fetish thing can sometimes feel like a cliché. How many female characters in movies and on TV have been defined by their all-consuming and adorable adoration of shoes? They're as excited as King Arthur pulling the magical sword out of the stone every time they happen upon a pair of great slingback sandals, and their life is forever changed by some cute peep-toe pumps. I'm not that insane about shoes, and neither are any of my friends. We're rational, flesh-and-blood people. We like shoes—sometimes we even lust after them—but we don't experience nirvana every time we happen upon a great pair. Well, maybe a little bit, if they're especially fantastic and reasonably priced.

For most of us, shoes are a necessary expense. You won't get served in some restaurants if you're not wearing any, and you'll probably get a horrible fungus and lose a limb if you go barefoot in most subways. And yeah, there are some people who prefer to go barefoot. They're the same people that make you take your shoes off when they throw a party, which is incredibly rude. Maybe tall people don't mind, but I'm 5'2" on a good day, if I stand on my tiptoes and stretch, and I want to wear my goddamn wedges at your party so I don't feel like a forest sprite every time I talk to someone taller than I am. Plus, they complete my outfit. I'm not a shoe maniac, but I do understand them and I know how to buy them, which is why you should deem me a worthy advisor when it comes to buying shoes. I might not understand or trust the stock market, but I feel supremely confident in my ability to spend wisely on footwear. Here are a few tricks:

1. Find a gorgeous pair of shoes.

2. Immediately check the price before putting them on your feet.

3. If they're beyond your budget, put them back. Why torture yourself? Step away.

4. Locate an amazing pair that's affordable and try those on instead.

5. If you're hobbling, limping, or have tiny tears coming out of your eyes, put them back. Can you imagine Audrey Hepburn teetering around in beautiful but painful shoes? No.

6. If it's a pair you'll wear for years, in all sorts of weather, it's OK to splurge. For example, if you skimp on winter boots you might wind up slipping in a blizzard and bruising your tailbone.

7. When the soles of your favorite shoes wear out, take them to a cobbler and, like magic (for a small amount of money) they'll be fixed.

I can dole out shoe-buying tips like a pro, but if you asked me for stock tips, you would be met with a stare so blank you'd think I'd been possessed by the spirits of Tila Tequila, Biff from *Back to the Future*, and Malibu Barbie. Actually, my stock market advice would be exactly the same as Mark Twain's:

> OCTOBER. *This is one of the particularly dangerous months to invest in stocks. Other dangerous months are July, January, September, April, November, May, March, June, December, August, and February.*[12]

I know people have made much more money buying and selling stocks than they have buying and selling shoes. I'm not counting Christian Louboutin, Jessica Simpson, or Manolo Blahnik. I also know that investing wisely can sometimes be a very savvy use of your money. If you're looking for a book brimming with stock tips that will make you a billionaire, you've probably gathered by now that this is not that.

Or maybe you are still looking for stock tips, in which case, here's one for you: the stock market can be as dangerous as it is exciting, as we know all too well from movies, daytime talk shows, and real life. I prefer to get my adrenaline rush doing something cool like sneaking into hotel pools or haggling at yard sales. The stock market is just too risky. Losing thousands or tens of thousands in a split second is not my idea of a good time. Splurging on a pair of badass black boots because you know you'll wear them and that they'll make you happy and confident is more my speed. Especially if you wear the boots until they disintegrate—that's called getting your money's worth.

I once knew a guy who made his living as a day trader. He was a regular at Seagull Feather Heaven. This guy ran his one-man operation out of a tiny studio apartment that was perched above the Venice boardwalk in Los Angeles. The intermingled scent of sage, patchouli, cigarettes, ocean air, and weed would float through the window as he worked, and his uniform of choice was one of those

---

12. Twain, Mark. *Pudd'nhead Wilson*. Charles L. Webster & Compootany, 1894.

Mexican ponchos that surfers and people who spend their days day trading inside a cloud of pot smoke sometimes wear. Despite what you might be assuming, I did not date this person. I've made a hell of a lot of mistakes, but a barefoot pothead hippie day trader was not one of them. Please, hold your applause.

I met this guy during my Post-College Existential Meltdown, an era in which I hung out with a lot of kindred spirits like drunk poets, lost souls, and disgruntled day traders. One day, I went over to the hippie stock broker's place after my lunch shift, and he tried to teach me about day trading. He'd been working all morning and his eyes were bugging out, so his energy could best be described as "demented and stressed," kind of like the people on Wall Street. He pointed to a bunch of stuff on his computer screen that made no sense to me, and he said a lot of things that I think were in English but that sounded like speaking in tongues. This often happens when I'm faced with extreme logic or math or words like "futures exchange": my eyes cross, my brain shrivels to the size of a single dust mote, and the world goes dark.

Once he stopped talking, my brain went back to normal and everything came back into focus. I did understand him when he said, "It's the coolest because one month I made $15,000. That's in one month, man. You can't make that at a desk job." Sometimes I can actually be logical, because I asked, "What's the most you've lost in a month?" He fiddled with the string on his poncho and mumbled, "Twenty grand. That was rough." His neck and face started to redden, and his eyes got that bulgy look again. It was not sexy. "Let's get some food," he said as he stood up and grabbed his skateboard. "I don't wanna get into it."

Of course he didn't. Who would? I can guarantee you no one has ever lost $20,000 in a month due to a shoe emergency—unless they lost a pair that cost that much, or they put money into a shoe company that tanked. Buying shoes and investing in the stock market are very different ways to spend your money, and they require very different skill sets and mental states. I just think that putting money into a fickle, unpredictable entity and betting that some app or the next iteration of chia seeds will make you rich is an extremely risky and bad way to spend your hard-earned cash. Buying a pair of shoes is much smarter. It costs less (hopefully), you can get everyday enjoyment out of them, and you don't have to worry about becoming apoplectic when you realize tens of thousands of dollars vanished, just like that. Instead, you can just stare down at your feet and rejoice.

31

LA MER IS LA MER

L a Mer. Moisturizer to the stars. A miracle cream that transforms your face and ages you backward, giving you the skin of Cate Blanchett or a five-week-old newborn. It was created by a visionary doctor to help your body renew itself, like a space alien or a butterfly bursting out of the cocoon.

For a few years I flipped through magazines showing ads for this mystical beauty product and wondered, "What's the deal with La Mer?" I knew it was pricy, so instead of running out and buying it, I'd just flip to the next page, where another glossy ad would assault my senses and prey upon my insecurities, leaving me to wonder what the deal was with Ralph Lauren's "mini Ricky" bag, Viktor & Rolf's Flowerbomb perfume, or Nivea's Skin Firming lotion. Every product that claims to zap cellulite and tone your skin turns me into a skeptic. Do they really do what they say they do? And if they did, wouldn't the world be cellulite free? Wouldn't we all be throwing ticker tape parades and sashaying through the streets in our underwear if they actually did what they promised? Actually, forget ticker tape parades. We'd just be posting selfies of the backs of our thighs and hashtagging #Nivea #blessed.

The fact that beauty is big business isn't exactly breaking news, and we all buy into the promise of clear, wrinkle-free skin with diminished pores to one degree or another. If I weren't careful, beauty products would be my downfall, financially speaking. Give me vanilla-fig lotion and a candle that smells like rhubarb, rain, and Moroccan amber, and I'm in heaven. I'd be bankrupted by things like brown-sugar-and-black-orchid-scented bath salts or whipped-coconut-and-almond body oil if I wasn't careful. I don't care about fancy cars or a house with fifteen bathrooms, but I do care about agave-plum lip masks and face mists made of cucumber essence and snow algae. Maybe that's why I love free samples so much.

La Mer was never on my shopping list, but one day, as I was wandering through Nordstrom getting my beauty fix by inhaling every Jo Malone scent in sight, from Wild Fig & Cassis to Oud & Bergamot to Wild Bluebell, a very nice salesperson told me they were giving out samples of La Mer. "Would you like one?" she asked. As if anyone in her right mind would decline. I'm a skeptic, but I still want to believe that there are miracle creams and potions out there, just like I'd like to believe that there is life on other planets and that they'll come hang with us soon and teach us how to lower the cost of gasoline and make all the bad stuff go away.

"Yes!" I said to the salesperson. Of course I wanted to try this magical mystery cream that all the stars swore by. They were probably paid to swear by it, but still. I thanked her for the sample and carefully placed the round thimble-sized plastic container into my bag. When she turned her back to me, I took a big whiff of some Peony & Blush Suede perfume and then headed off with my loot.

Once I got home, it was time to put La Mer to the test. Each night and morning for two weeks, I'd twist off the little white cap and apply a pea-sized dollop of lotion to my face. The sample truly was the size of a thimble, so if I was about to experience a miracle I wanted it to last. After applying the cream I'd walk down my foot-long hallway to bed, imagining that this was what it was like to be Nicole Kidman or Halle Berry on a Tuesday night, going to sleep with a supernatural phenomenon working its magic on my skin. I was ready to be wowed. I was ready for a miracle.

You might not believe this, but after two weeks, when I'd scraped the last infinitesimal blob of lotion out of the microscopic plastic pot and applied it to my cheeks, it was not Cate Blanchett's alabaster visage that stared back at me in the mirror. It was still my slightly ruddy mug. Maybe I needed more time, and more La Mer. Maybe I needed more faith to make it work. All I know is that a miracle did not occur, which wasn't too upsetting since I didn't invest any money in my experiment. If I'd paid up, I'd have been pretty sad. And we all know that sadness and stress are terrible for your complexion.

Maybe gently spreading La Mer over your skin in a clockwise motion is better than rubbing a stick of butter over your face before bed, but, despite what the magazines say, you don't have to spend thousands of dollars on creams and lotions and gels and microalgae oils. You just need to get really good at scoring free samples. All you have to do is ask. There is no reason for you to pine for pricey beauty products. But if the samples don't work or if you're living in a redwood tree and have no access to Sephora, there are some old-school beauty tricks that work just as well as La Mer.

Our grandparents had cold cream, witch hazel, and talcum powder, and they were fine. It's not like people in the 1940s and 1950s were running around town looking like a circus sideshow act just because La Mer hadn't been invented yet. My grandmother was always put-together and beautiful, and she used cold cream, witch hazel, and pink sponge curlers as part of her beauty routine. I can still hear her sweet Southern voice in my head to this day, saying, "Don't ever leave the house with chipped nail polish or you'll look like a two-bit whore." That's solid beauty advice if I've ever heard it.

Granted, you'd be hard-pressed to give a beauty product a name as aggressive and scary as "witch hazel," but that stuff stands the test of time. It's an old-school astringent, and you can still buy it at drug stores for about five bucks. The only downside is that it smells just like it sounds: like an ancient, toothless, shriveled up ogress. If you can get past that, you'll love it.

There are plenty of home remedies and cheap beauty fixes that involve honey, oatmeal, egg yolks, beer, and Brewer's yeast. They might not come in pretty packages and have ingredients like tourmaline, Meadowfoam, and *Phaseolus lunatus* (lima bean) extract, but they can still make you feel fabulous without wiping out your bank account. Using raw honey as a face mask works wonders. Jojoba oil, which is about seven bucks for four ounces, lasts a long time, and if you use that as your eye makeup remover/elbow oil/miracle hand salve, you'll feel rejuvenated and revitalized and all those other adjectives the chichi products use but for a lot less.

When I was in eighth grade I read a magazine article that said everyone should finish every shower with freezing cold water like French women do because it will tighten your pores and keep you looking young and fresh forever. I've been finishing each shower with icy water every single day of my life since then, and I don't know if it's working but I do know that it gives me hope, despite the fact that I'm spending ten seconds freezing my face off each day.

Our parents and grandparents had movie magazines and beauty ads bombarding them with miracle products too, but it wasn't as extreme back then. They had chinstraps (the economical face lift of the 1950s) and weird callisthenic workout routines, but there was no Botox, microdermabrasion, or chemical peels. Now we have all that plus so much more, making it so tempting to compare yourself to an ad in a magazine or a celeb on a red carpet. That comparison is not healthy, considering that we'd all look impeccable, toned, and well rested if our every move was airbrushed and our daily schedule went like this:

9:00 AM: Rise to the sound of little birds chirping on the lawn

9:15 AM: Ring a bell and wait until your assistant Babette arrives with a kale-and-bone-marrow-broth smoothie

10:00 AM: Yoga and meditation

12:00 PM: Lounge by pool and get a massage from Jean-Pierre the tanning butler as a string quartet plays nearby

2:00 PM: Private SoulCycle class

3:30 PM: Ring a bell and wait for Babette to arrive with the heirloom-tofu-and-beet salad

4:00 PM: Facial, manicure, pedicure

5:00 PM: Read *Vogue*

7:00 PM: Dinner and dancing!

10:00 PM: Take off makeup, apply La Mer, and fall immediately into a deep sleep for eight hours in which you age backwards, become smarter, and learn four languages

Most of us don't have that exact schedule, so we do want to believe in the creams and gels and under-eye depuffing serums advertised in the pages of glossy magazines. If the pricy products aren't yet within your budget, you can still have a beauty routine that makes you feel like Venus de Milo or J. Lo. You could even try making your own La Mer by taking a bunch of seaweed and smashing it (gently) all over your face, but I'm not sure that'll work. If not, there are always freezing-cold showers, raw honey, and that most glorious invention of all: the free sample.

32

THE NEIMAN MARCUS EXPERIMENT

Remember the Stanford "marshmallow test?" The one where a psychologist named Walter Mischel took a bunch of little kids and gave them each a single marshmallow, told them they could eat it right away or else wait until the grown-up came back into the room, but if they waited they'd get an extra marshmallow?[13] If you didn't know about it before, you do now. Bring it up at your next cocktail party. You'll be big a hit.

In this experiment, some of the kids ate the single marshmallow right away, some tried to wait but then couldn't help themselves, and some waited patiently to earn the second marshmallow when the adult came back into the room. The study proved that some kids are greedy little bastards, and some aren't. And that's not all. Mischel then tracked the kids over time into adulthood, and found that the ones who waited patiently and didn't jam the first marshmallow into their yappers got better grades, were more successful in their careers, and were healthier overall than the impulsive kids who ate the glucose globule right away. Therefore, having willpower and patience makes you a happier, more well-adjusted person. Life is more complex than a marshmallow though, and maybe some of those kids just thought squishy white cubes of

---

13 . "Cognitive and attentional mechanisms in delay of gratification." Mischel, Walter; Ebbesen, Ebbe B.; Raskoff Zeiss, Antonette Journal of Personality and Social Psychology, Vol 21(2), Feb 1972, 204-218. http://dx.doi.org/10.1037/h0032198

sugar were icky, but the results are interesting nonetheless.

There's a reason for all this talk about marshmallows. It begins and ends with Neiman Marcus, the luxury department store filled with thousands of marshmallows in the form of 18 karat Gold Polished Rock Candy Cutout Linear Station necklaces, diamond-and-ruby ladybug pendants, and $25,000 silk organza Valentino ball gowns.

My grandmother was a real fashionista who wore pink ostrich feather dresses and occasionally rocked a silk turban. She used to stroll me through the Neiman Marcus in Fort Worth, Texas, when I was an infant, so maybe that's when my fascination with the place began. One second though—I should clarify two things before we continue:

1. My grandmother sometimes wore silk turbans, but she did not eat cat food out of a tin à la Big and Little Edie. She ate tuna salad sandwiches and blueberry pie at Continental Cafeteria, off of plates.

2. This is not the same grandmother who used witch hazel and pink sponge curlers.

Now that we're clear on that, let's go back to Neiman's. Because I'm an ace anthropologist, I sometimes like to go deep undercover and stroll through the hallowed aisles of the Beverly Hills Neiman Marcus just to get a glimpse of some Valentino ball gowns and the rarefied creatures that buy them. The store is a beautiful place, a real-life Shangri-La. It's always impeccably clean and shiny, and it has no smell. Have you ever noticed that? Neiman Marcus is odorless, as if it exists in a beautiful vacuum of purity and sanitation. How do they keep it so immaculate, without a trace of Pine-Sol or Windex lingering in the air? It's a miracle, really. I'm sure if you walked through the cosmetics department as someone sprayed a cloud of Lolita Lempicka Eau de Parfum in your path it would be a different story, but mostly it's aroma-free.

It's not as if I go sleuthing in Neiman's once a week or anything. Both driving and walking in Beverly Hills are extremely dangerous activities, and I try to avoid them as much as possible. You're surrounded by a bunch of mean old drivers who don't care if they whack you with the door of their Bentley or run you down on their way to a mani-pedi appointment. Still, I have been known to brave Beverly Hills on occasion. It's like going to the zoo or to a carnival, just without any rides or mirth or churros.

Walking around Neiman Marcus is entertaining, but it also makes me feel like a criminal. I just know the security guards and salespeople are eyeballing my every move, ready to cuff me just in case I stuff a Burberry scarf down my shirt and run toward the door. I'm probably being slightly paranoid, but that's how it feels. Maybe it's just a defense mechanism. If I waltzed in there and felt right-at-home enough to just charge some Jimmy Choo pumps and a few handbags to my credit card, I'd be in big trouble. This is where the marshmallow test comes in.

If you're able to waltz into Neiman's (or Barneys or Saks or Bergdorf's), snap your fingers, and have your personal shopper, Fredo, suddenly appear with a rack of couture gowns, then good for you and please enjoy it. If not, and if charging a bunch of stuff at Neiman's is financially irresponsible, you need to think of the marshmallow test, and you need to exercise some willpower. Step away from the soft leather boxy jacket and the La Perla Maharani Lace Embellished Bodysuit for $904. Give it a day or two. Maybe in the morning you won't even remember lusting after those things.

> **Step away from the soft leather boxy jacket and the La Perla Maharani Lace Embellished Bodysuit for $904. Give it a day or two.**

If, on the other hand, you've taken some time to think about it and you've realized that you *can* buy that bodysuit, and that you won't be going into debt or jeopardizing your I Didn't See This Shit Coming Fund for your car (this is $904 we're talking about, not $94), then go back and get yourself two marshmallows. In this case, two marshmallows = one bodysuit. Willpower is important when you're shopping, especially at a place like Neiman Marcus.

Sometimes, though, shopping on a whim is fun, and life would be boring and extremely annoying if every time you wanted a new skirt you had to draw pie charts and ponder every single purchase as if you were Cleopatra contemplating sending a fleet of ships into battle. If it's a pricy purchase, I usually walk around whatever store I'm in for a while instead of immediately buying it, just to make sure I really like it. More often than not, I end up sticking whatever I was holding back on the rack and strutting out of the store like a badass because I saved some money and I'm feeling invincible. You can always return things too. It's not like it's 42 BC, when people were beheaded for siding with plebeians and there were no return policies at department stores.

The very first day I went sleuthing, I met a very sweet sales guy in the housewares section of Neiman's who told me all kinds of stories about the princesses and celebrities who pop in and buy twenty-piece china sets and Chantilly lace tablecloths as nonchalantly as the rest of us buy a case of Bounty paper towels at Costco. He's now my Deep Throat—my mole on the inside. I haven't learned anything scandalous yet, so I'm not sure that anything especially insane ever happens at Neiman Marcus, but I've got my ear to the ground. If you do find yourself wandering through the store on the verge of a panic attack because you're stressed about work or rent or life in general, and you're contemplating either screaming and causing a scene or buying a rose quartz necklace you probably shouldn't be buying, just close your eyes and say the code word: MARSHMALLOWS.

And then mosey on over to Marshalls. You're far less likely to have a financial and/or emotional meltdown there.

33

CAN'T AFFORD A TAILOR?
A STAPLER WORKS JUST FINE

A ll through my twenties I bounced from corporate job to server job and back again in a seemingly never-ending loop. I'd go for the corporate jobs because I'd get sick of busting my ass for tips, working weekends, and paying (or not) for my own health insurance, and then I'd run to the restaurant jobs when I needed freedom from the air-conditioned nightmare and the cubicle and the kitchenette drawers full of sporks. This manic career trajectory happened in two-year cycles: two years serving omelets, two years copyediting tech news. Your career is a marathon, not a sprint, goes the old cliché, so for the first decade of my working life I was basically an ultra-runner, minus the endorsement deals and glory and strong ropey gams.

The first job in this workaday merry-go-round was at an entertainment company in Los Angeles, right after college. To give you a sense of the level of corporate-ness we're dealing with here, everyone who has come into contact with this company calls it the Death Star. My job was so insignificant there really wasn't a name for it. I wasn't "on a desk," which is the Hollywood way of saying I wasn't an assistant sitting in a cubicle getting screamed at by the boss whenever a call drops or a latte gets cold. I was one rung below that, stuffed into a windowless, broom-closet sized room with a guy named Paul, logging screenplays and daydreaming about Henry Miller and Paris cafés. A Paris café seemed like the height of sophistication and coolness to me then. It also seemed a hell of a lot better than logging scripts in a broom closet.

Paul was a wannabe musician and I was a wannabe writer, so we were fast friends. We drew yellow suns and white puffy clouds and trees and rainbows on printer paper and hung them on the wall of the broom closet so we could at least have some pretend windows to look at. We had hope, and we also thought our fake windows might help us keep any potential career-related or claustrophobia-induced panic attacks at bay. It worked, for the most part. I did have a minor panic attack in that room one day when I came back from lunch and realized there was a doughnut-shaped welt on my throat because a bee had stung me. I hadn't noticed until I got back to the broom closet, when Paul looked at me as if I'd returned from lunch looking like Jar Jar Binks and blurted, "Holy shit—what's wrong with you?!" I'd never been stung by a bee before, so I was convinced I was going to puff up like Martin Short in *Pure Luck* and then die inside the Death Star. Instead, a doctor gave me some Claritin and told me to go back to work. I kind of wanted him to confirm my fears and rush me into surgery so I wouldn't have to go back there, but sadly that didn't happen.

One tricky thing about working at the Death Star—and about any corporate job—is making sure you have a suitable wardrobe for work, which is likely completely opposite to what you wear in your normal life, unless you love wearing lame pantsuits, pastel cardigans, and Ann Taylor dresses. If you're a peon who has to create your own windows out of printer paper like Paul and I were, you're barely making enough to live, so it's hard to shop anywhere except Buffalo Exchange or Target. You can get corporate outfits at Target, but man are they lame.

Since this was my first "real" job, I hadn't yet figured out how to make my normal clothes and my cubicle/broom-closet clothes merge as one. As soon as I'd get home from work I'd fling off my cheapo charcoal grey polyester and cotton pants and "presentable" top and pull on a vintage bowling shirt that had the name PHIL B. embroidered across the pocket, along with some denim shorts. In case you're horrified, I would tie the baggy PHIL B. shirt in a knot at the waist to make it look stylish and vaguely sexy, thank you very much. I have no idea who Phil was, but I'm sure he would have appreciated the way I styled his old bowling shirt.

Maybe I was at war with my Death Star wardrobe because I was at war with the job. That's part of it. It was also just an ugly wardrobe. If you do have to pay for an entire corporate set of clothes that you would never wear outside of work because they make you look and feel like an L.L.Bean mannequin, you need to get creative and sneaky with your purchases. Find a pair of black pants that can look dronish when paired with a crisp button-down but cool when matched with an old Sonic Youth concert tee. Make sure that crisp button-down can be tied in a knot and worn with some jeans as well. I'm big on tying tops at the waist in case you can't tell. Oprah says it's good to have a signature style, so maybe that's mine.

Another problem with work clothes is the maintenance. Taking things to the cleaners adds up, and if you toss your sheath dress and suit jacket in the wash with your dishrags and socks, you'll eventually ruin them. If you're a shorty like I am, you also have to pay to have every single pair of pants and jeans hemmed, which I believe is some sort of conspiracy. Is it that hard to make pants for people who are 5'3" and under? Someone needs to get to the bottom of this. No pun intended. For real. I'm not big on puns.

> *Find a pair of black pants that can look dronish when paired with a crisp button-down but cool when matched with an old Sonic Youth concert tee.*

Besides having ugly clothes, I had one major wardrobe malfunction at the Death Star that taught me valuable lessons about clothes, finances, integrity, and the nature of hierarchy. It happened one afternoon when Paul was off running around the building, delivering scripts to red-faced agents whose temperaments suggested they began each day by downing an elixir of carrot juice, Grey Goose vodka, and bile. As I was staring at the floor and thinking about Paris cafés, I noticed that the hem of my charcoal grey polyester and cotton pants had come undone. Full of ennui, I contemplated what to do about it. I had been at the Death Star for nearly a year, and paying to have those pants hemmed seemed unbearable, as if the decision to take them to the tailor signified something. I don't know what—that I'd given up on life? That the universe was melting? That I was cheap? I'm still not sure. I was infatuated with Paris at the time, which spiked every thought I had with pretention and tragedy.

What I am sure about is that I pulled myself up out of the chair, summoned all of my strength, walked the two steps it took to get to the table in the center of the broom closet with all the office supplies on it, hoisted my leg onto the table, grabbed the jumbo-sized stapler, and started stapling the hem of my pants. If you didn't just picture that happening in slow motion, I suggest you reread it and imagine it that way. It adds a touch of drama, and I think you'll understand my mental state at that time much better if everything is in slow motion.

Back in real time, as I was just about to click the last staple in place, my boss walked into the broom closet holding a stack of scripts. There she was, looking professional in her corporate casual pantsuit, and there I was, stapling my pants hem with one leg hiked up on the table like a common hobo. She froze and I froze. What else do you do in this situation? Put your leg down like a normal person? That would have been a good move.

She handed me the stack of scripts and said, "I need these logged ASAP." I finally pulled my leg down, took the scripts, and started to explain why I was stapling my pants, but she just turned on her heels and walked out the door. I'm not sure she even saw me, to tell you the truth, which says a lot about my position at the company. She kind of looked through me, like those people you talk to who seem like they're looking at your forehead or your ear or off to the side at the blank nothingness beyond.

It was embarrassing, and I don't recommend the experience. You can't know everything at your first job, and you also probably can't afford to tailor fifteen decent corporate casual outfits if you're an intern or an entry-level peon. But you can try and find a way to make your real clothes and your bullshit clothes work harmoniously together as one. You can also learn to sew a hem and patch a tear without the help of a stapler. You don't have to buy patterns and make it complicated, but it's amazing what you can learn about sewing a hem from YouTube videos and Lifehacker. Plus, threading a needle is a great exercise in patience. It can be very Zen, as long as you don't lose your mind. You can also try those "self-threading needles," which sound amazing but seem like an urban myth.

And, as you're threading those needles and hemming your ugly corporate slacks, if you keep forging ahead, even when you're full of ennui and life feels like it's going in slow motion, the clothes and the jobs will get better. And if you do find yourself in a pickle and need to hem your pants with staples, just go do it in a bathroom stall or in a dark corner where no one can see you. It's much more professional.

34

HOW TO BUY A $10 PRESSED JUICE
AND NOT FEEL LIKE AN ASSHOLE

"I really appreciate you."

That's a very sweet thing to say to a family member or a good friend or an employee who just went the extra mile. It's a wise thing to say to the person you love when they're driving you nuts and you want to communicate something more peaceful than, "Would it kill you to take the dishes out of the washer just once?!" or "We need to work as a team so listen to me and turn right, goddamnit!" It is, however, a weird thing to say to the person who just charged you $9.50 for a pressed juice. See:

> **Salesperson:** *"Here's your Turmeric Alkalizer juice. That'll be $9.50."*
>
> **Customer:** *"I really appreciate you."*

Standing one day in my local pressed-juice place waiting to order an Acai Summertime Cleanser, I overheard the grey-haired gentleman in front of me thus overzealously thanking the twenty-something juice barista who sold it to him. I already felt like an asshole just being there amongst the fat-burning limeade and raw organic doggie treats, and this guy just made it worse. I guess I didn't feel guilty enough, though, because when he left, which he did after first staring meaningfully into the juice barista's eyes and penetrating her soul with his appreciation, I stepped up and ordered my own overpriced tonic.

Much like with La Mer, thoughts like "What is the deal with pressed juice?" used to occupy my thoughts more than they should. Maybe it's because I live in a city where ten-buck carrot/beet/turmeric puree is as normal as a five-cent Cherry Coke was in the 1950s. It's easy to make fun of the ridiculously overpriced juice craze—I do it all the time. But you know what? Sometimes you just want a Phytonutrient Cilantro Fennel Detox drink. Like beauty products, pressed juice gives us hope. Hope that it will cure what ails us (like a hangover or a bad-hair day), rejuvenate our bodies, and cause our skin to glow within seconds of consuming it. Fancy juices won't kill you, unless you go overboard and OD on spirulina or cacao nibs, and they're definitely better for you than a Big Mac or a deep-fried Oreo. Still, they're pricey. And, let's just be honest—they're a little ridiculous.

If you do find yourself zombie-walking into a juice place because you have a sudden craving for liquid kale, there are a few things you can do to avoid sending yourself into a spiral of financial guilt and shame when the last sip of your pressed juice has been slurped. For starters, getting your own juicer and making concoctions at home will save you money in the long run. If that's not happening, or if you just can't bring yourself to make your own juice that day because the thought of spending half an hour cleaning the thing is too agonizing, just make sure you don't tell the juice barista that you appreciate them, unless you're in a relationship with them or they're a blood relative. On the other hand, if they give

> *Sometimes you just want a Phytonutrient Cilantro Fennel Detox drink. Like beauty products, pressed juice gives us hope.*

you a wink and say, "This one's on the house," it's OK to tell them you appreciate them.

Other than that, here are a few tricks to help you buy an over-priced pressed juice without feeling like an asshole:

Make peace with your decision. Accept the fact that you are about to spend too much money on liquefied grass and spices. Promise not to beat yourself up. After all, we spend that much money on cocktails. The occasional juice is a lot better for you, just probably not as fun.

Buy only in moderation. If, like with coffee, paying nine bucks for a juice every day will jeopardize your savings or your finances, make it a special-occasion thing. Like if you have a big date or a big kickball game that night and you think some goji berries and maca powder will make you invincible, knock yourself out.

Get something exotic. If you're going to do this, do it all the way. Don't overspend on something boring like a carrot apple juice that you can make at home. Get CoQ10, "fruits of the earth," and "E3Live" in that thing. I don't know what any of that does, but at least you'll be living on the edge, for just one dollar more.

Never speak of it again. There is nothing more boring than listening to someone blab about their diet or their detox regime. I would rather sit through a lecture on the history of cardboard than hear someone talk about how many pounds they've lost by drinking a pressed juice. Drink your juice, accept what you've just done, and never speak of it again. No one needs to know. Except maybe your nutritionist, if you have one of those.

So there you have it. Four easy steps to help you shake off the guilt and enjoy your cold pressed juice. It's got more juice and nutrients in it than Five Alive or SunnyD, so at least you've got that going for you. Plus, you have to choose your battles in life, and getting angry about Green Garden smoothies and kale-beet puree is a real waste of time and energy. It's not as if pressed juice is part of some holistic food conspiracy. At the end of the day, it's just juice. Just don't get overzealous with the stuff. Balance it out with a hamburger or some fries here and there. That's called being well-rounded.

35

SHARE WITH YOUR FRIENDS, ESPECIALLY THE ONES WITH BETTER CLOTHES

The idea of sharing clothes with your friends:

A. Sounds promising

B. Fills you with dread

C. Is something you do all the time because it's fun and financially savvy

D. Makes you want to lock your entire wardrobe in a Swiss bank vault and swallow the key

E. Both B & D

According to years of extensive research by Yours Truly, PhD, the correct answers are, of course, A and C. If you answered B, D, or E, it could either be because of your vile and selfish nature or because you grew up with annoying, shifty siblings who had no concept of privacy, decency, or personal property. If you had given me this pop quiz when I was between the ages of eleven and eighteen,

I would have circled B, D, and E, several times, in red pen, until the ink ran out. Then I would have torn the paper into a hundred pieces, stomped on the shreds, and set them on fire. Not because I was demonic (even though we're all a little demonic at that age), but because I was living in a house with three younger sisters who did not understand or acknowledge my physical, mental, and overall dominance in the hierarchy of our lives. I am the oldest; therefore I reign supreme. That's just a fact. My sisters were the demons and I was the innocent victim.

In case you think I was (and still am) overreacting, let me try and generate a little empathy. I'll merge all three sisters into one composite, cloven-footed character and name it Helga. A typical morning before school in our house went like this:

DG: *Where are my green suede shoes?!*

Helga: *I don't know.*

DG: *And where are my overalls? They were right here last night!*

Helga: *I haven't seen them.*

DG: *YES YOU HAVE!*

Helga: *NO I HAVEN'T!*

That would be my cue to open Helga's closet and look on the ground under a heap of discarded pants and shirts. Without fail I would end up pulling out my green suede shoes and overalls as she stood behind me holding my brush and backpack and jean jacket behind her back, swearing she hadn't touched any of my things.

DG: *I knew it! Stop taking my clothes!*

Helga: *I didn't take them.*

DG: *YES YOU DID!*

Helga: *I don't know how they got there!*

DG: *GET OUT OF MY LIFE I HATE YOU!*

Helga: *I HATE YOU TOO!*

And then we'd hate each other for about four minutes, go to school, and do the whole thing again the next day. It was exhausting, and as you can tell from my meticulously reconstructed dialogue, we hadn't mastered the whole communication thing yet, so we were caught in a never-ending cycle of love, hate, and closet pillaging. There's something nice about this Neanderthal-type communication, though. It's primal and real. Eventually, however, you have to grow up, speak in complete sentences, and engage in civilized discussions about the things that irk you. Unless you're a reality TV star. If that's the case it's advisable and even expected that you act like a drunk, deranged Neanderthal at all times.

The clothes sound hideous now, but I adored those lime green suede shoes with tasseled laces. I would sometimes pair them with white cotton tights, forest green wool shorts, a white T-shirt, and a floral denim jacket. Plop a feathered cap on me and I'd be Peter Pan, but the wannabe grunge version. As if that elfin ensemble weren't bad enough, in eleventh grade I was obsessed with a burgundy crushed velvet catsuit complete with stirrups at the feet. I paired it with some black flats and wore it every chance I got: the Homecoming dance, a Bar Mitzvah, while sitting at home watching *Beverly Hills, 90210* with Helga, pretending to do my math homework. The pièce de résistance in my wardrobe was my beloved black cap embellished with sequined elephants that I got at Pier 1. Looking back, maybe Helga was doing me a favor by stealing and hiding my clothes, but at the time it felt like sabotage.

Unless you're fine throwing on brown pants and a brown smock every day of your life, your clothes have meaning. They're expressions of who you are, what you feel, and what you want to telegraph to the world. Some people don't like or care about clothes, and they're probably the same people who don't like movies or water. Haven't you ever met those people who are all, "I don't like water" or "I don't like movies"? They're probably the same people who walk around in brown smocks. Or else they're soulless aliens. How can you not like water? I find those people very suspicious.

Even if you're in a T-shirt and jeans, it's probably a T-shirt and jeans that you feel says to the world: "This outfit is who I am and what I represent and I think my ass looks pretty good in it too!" When you grow up and you start communicating beyond those three magic words "I HATE YOU" and realize that those shirts and tops that have meaning are also expensive, you'll come to see that sharing clothes with people can be fun. It can also save you hundreds of dollars. Chances are you have at least one friend or sibling who is your same size who doesn't dress in Crocs and that most horrible of inventions, drop-crotch pants. I tried on a pair of drop-crotch pants one day because they were trendy and I thought maybe, just maybe, I could rock them. I stepped out of the dressing room looking like I'd just leapt off the pages of a Dr. Seuss book and landed in a Diesel store. Maybe I would have worn them back in high school, but because I've grown older and wiser and am less inclined to dress like a fictional animated character, I put the drop-crotch pants back on the rack and never looked back.

When it comes to sharing, find friends who have similar taste in clothing. Trade with them. Start a barter system. Let their closet be your Neiman Marcus, and your closet can be their . . . Marshalls. If your friends are nice, decent people, they'll be happy to share their stuff. If they're not, they probably haven't dealt with the memory of their siblings stealing their clothes yet.

Say you splurge on a piece of special-occasion clothing you love, and you're walking around feeling guilty because you've worn it only once and it's just sitting in your closet. Let your friends borrow it, which will help you feel less guilty about your purchase. If they're going to their fifteenth wedding of the year or a lame cocktail party for work and they're in need of a free outfit, open your closet to them. If you can't tolerate the thought of anyone else wearing your $300 Alice + Olivia minidress or your rag & bone paisley tie, you can hang them on your closet door like a piece of art in a museum so you can bask in their beauty on a daily basis, thus getting your money's worth *psychologically.*

If you're burned-out on garage sales, you can also get a bunch of friends together and have a clothes-swap party, which basically means you all bring the clothes you don't want anymore, drink wine, and trade with each other. By the end of the night you have a new, free wardrobe. Don't drink too much though, or you might wake up the next morning to find a crushed red velvet catsuit and some green suede shoes with tassels in your closet. I'm sure that old catsuit is hanging in a Goodwill in Texas somewhere, giving people a good laugh. Or maybe someone is wearing it right this second, asserting her individuality and admiring the stirrup feet like I once did. I just hope that person likes water and movies, and I hope she's able to share that exquisite piece of fashion history with her friends.

36

ZEN AND THE ART
OF BANKRUPTCY

The universe is teeming with spiritual people. Take Los Angeles—a certifiable mecca of spirituality, that is, if the certification comes from Tony Robbins or a buff dude named Bodhi who suffers from "sex addiction." It's a fact—every male yoga teacher in L.A. is Charlie Sheen in Lululemon pants. They might not all look like Charlie Sheen, but they resemble him inside, where it counts.

Despite all that, spirituality is great. It certainly beats being a cold shell of a person. You can let go of all worldly possessions, become a monk, and go live on a mountaintop like Leonard Cohen did—but then again, who wants to do that? It sounds pretty lonely. You can't tweet; you can't watch your favorite TV shows. I doubt there's any sushi, Korean barbeque, or pressed juice up there. It is cheap though, once you pay for the transportation to get you to the mountaintop. If you're dedicated enough to truly check out and go on a spiritual quest, that's wonderful. Namaste and hallelujah to you.

Of course, you don't need a mountaintop to seek nirvana, not when there's reflexology and chakra healing and Reiki practice on pretty much every block. But, like most things in life, spiritual health doesn't come cheap, and not everyone can eat, pray, and love their way into blessed enlightenment. When I turned to therapy after leaving my boyfriend of seven years—the one I shared the tin apartment with in Brooklyn—the fee of $125 bucks a session nearly gave me a nervous breakdown. I did it for a while, but then, like many people, I had to find other ways to cope so I wouldn't go broke. For example, if you're stressed out and you can't afford a massage, then a glass of wine, a bloodcurdling scream, and an episode of *American Pickers* will do. It doesn't have to be *American Pickers* if that doesn't set your being aflame. Substitute anything you want. I just find a show about two grown men rooting around in hoarders' stashes of junk until they find a samurai sword or an old gas can pretty soothing. It puts things in perspective: you may be down at the moment, but at least you're not hoarding old seesaws and balls of twine for no reason.

Maybe you'd rather cut the cable cord and the wine and spend that money on healing sessions and reflexology. If so, that's your choice and that's great. My prescription may not be the most Zen, but it works for me. Spend your money in a way that suits you. If you can do without *Game of Thrones* and *Three's Company* reruns, and if reflexology makes you happier than a glass of cabernet, more power to you. I just feel like I can knead my own feet if I really need to, and watching Jack Tripper's endless pratfalls lifts my spirits and makes me feel whole again. It's not cleansing my internal organs and ridding me of toxins, but I'm OK with that.

> **If you're stressed out and you can't afford a massage, then a glass of wine, a bloodcurdling scream, and an episode of American Pickers *will do.***

Maybe I'm skeptical about pricey new-agey treatments because my experiences with them haven't been so hot. I'm not talking about the kind of spirituality where you're sitting on the beach quietly, feeling peaceful and at one with the waves. I mean the kind of spirituality where they charge you. That kind is very popular in Los Angeles, as you can imagine. There's yoga (which we could divide into endless factions like Modo and Bikram), meditation, intuitive energy classes, Vedic astrology, ecstatic dance classes, aura healing, Kabbalah, cupping therapy (not to be confused with couple's therapy), and SoulCycle, which is just about the least spiritual activity I have ever participated in.

I have a friend who loves SoulCycle, and it really is a release for her. It's a great workout. It takes place in a dark, windowless room that feels like it's heated to ninety degrees. With electro-country music blaring, you're crammed in with fifty strangers all pedaling as if they were being chased by a pack of rabid wolves. It burns calories, but soulful it is not. I've tried it twice and both times I left feeling like my soul had just been trapped inside a Boggle shaker. My ass looked great, but my spirit was rattled. Maybe you love this kind of thing and have no problem budgeting for the classes, which are about $34 a pop. I'm just very sensitive to loud noises and culty activities, so I'd rather not pay people to scream, "You are a BADASS! NAMASTE YOU LITTLE NINJAS!" over the Avicii blasting from the speakers.

SoulCycle is nothing compared to my most challenging spiritual experience, which happened in 2010 when I agreed to a date that required me to endure a three-hour meditation class, which is 10,800 seconds of meditation, in case you were wondering. And it was only my second date with this dude. This is not very spiritual of me, but the reason I agreed to the meditation date was because he was hot. I probably would have gone unicycling naked if he'd suggested it.

He was an ex–college football player and his name was The Sequoia. He never knew that though. "He's just so tall and strong and . . . he's like a sequoia," I said to my friend Kate over cocktails one night as I relayed every detail of our first date. The name stuck, and now I was breaking all kinds of rules and wearing sweatpants on a meditation date with The Sequoia. I did get cute Victoria's Secret sweatpants for the occasion, of course. It's important to look your best, even when you're doing deep-breathing exercises in hopes of entering a portal through your third eye.

The class took place in a converted church, and our meditation leader was a ponytailed man clad in black lace bellbottoms and a red silk shirt. He went by the name Narasimha. His real name was probably Donald or Toby, but he wanted to be called Narasimha, and we were there to open our souls, not nitpick.

I'm a modern woman, but I should have seen the light when we walked into the church and The Sequoia said, "Do you have cash? It's fifteen bucks." I guess I was still enamored by his sturdy good looks because I paid, found a pillow to sit on, and hoped for the best.

What transpired over the next 10,800 seconds was nothing short of miraculous. We shut our eyes and listened to a frizzy-haired guy in a billowy button-down playing a drum. Then Narasimha had us stand and jump up and down as if we were on pogo sticks, this time to the sound of the didgeridoo *and* the drum. Maybe the jumping was supposed to jostle our brains around and open us up to something spiritual. As a kid, when you close your eyes, hold your arms out, and spin in circles until you fall over, your head gets fuzzy and it feels pretty neat. I think Narasimha was having us do the adult version of that.

Once we were properly jostled, it was time to breathe through our third eye, which, in case you're not familiar, is located smack dab in the center of your forehead. We were instructed to focus. Our eyes were closed but I could feel The Sequoia's presence in the room and I really wanted to impress him, since I was sure he could feel my presence too. I needed to master this forehead breathing so he could one day tell our children, "Kids, I knew your mom was the one when I felt her mastering the third-eye chakra breathing that night in her sexy sweatpants." While this fantasy floated through my consciousness, I forced my attention back to my forehead. "Imagine a cool beam of light emanating out of your third eye," said Narasimha. "Feel the light moving in . . . and out . . ."

Maybe I have a knack for third-eye breathing because all of a sudden I felt a cool tunnel of air moving in and out of my forehead. Everything was going great for a while, but since hypochondria runs in my family I soon lost focus, became paranoid, and imagined that my soul was about to be sucked out into another dimension. Which dimension would it land in exactly? Would it hang out there for two minutes, or two hours? What if it liked that other dimension better and never returned? I was used to having my soul around. It wasn't so bad and I definitely didn't want to lose it. Eventually, by sheer force of will I pushed away those thoughts and allowed my lust for The Sequoia to keep me rooted. I managed to finish the third-eye meditation with my soul intact.

Then, mere seconds later, the didgeridoo bellowed and Narasimha had each of us move to the center of the room one at a time, eyes closed, so he could "pull the bad energy away" from us. When my turn came I blindly wandered to where I thought the center of the room was.

I could have been in the men's bathroom for all I knew. It didn't matter. I wanted Narasimha to pull the bad energy out of me. He made swishing sounds and grazed my body with his hands, which is pretty gross, but at the time it felt very spiritual. "Swoosh!" he said as he orbited around me. I wondered if The Sequoia could see me in his mind's eye. As Narasimha did whatever he was doing, the last remaining particles of cynicism melted away from my being and I felt hopeful. If a dude in lace bellbottoms could make everything better, taking all the bad energy away for the bargain-basement price of fifteen bucks, that seemed like a pretty good deal to me.

As we walked to the car after class, The Sequoia told me that I might "feel kind of funny" for a few days. "You might have mood swings or feel really depressed, but then it's like this euphoric state after. Make sure you drink a shitload of water." How sweet. He was worried about my hydration. We made out a little and talked about how great we felt thanks to the bouncing and forehead breathing we'd endured in the class. Then we made out some more, to the sounds of The Sequoia's favorite band. Phish.

When I woke up the next day, it felt like business as usual to me, spiritually speaking. I kept waiting for that drastic emotional response The Sequoia had predicted. I followed his advice and drank a shitload of water in anticipation of some cataclysmic comedown, but really the only comedown I experienced was when, over the course of the next few weeks, The Sequoia turned out to be a serial texter. You know, the ones whose texts go like this:

Sequoia: *Hey*

DG: *Hi!*

Sequoia: *What're you up to this weekend*

DG: *Not sure, maybe a party Friday nothing Saturday yet. What about you?*

and then . . . silence.
Or this:

DG: *How're things?*

Sequoia: *Cool. Wanna hang soon?*

DG: *Sure. Sunday?*

. . . and then silence again. These exchanges went on for a while before I gave up and realized that The Sequoia wasn't very spiritual at all, at least not like I imagined Ewan McGregor or Paul Newman probably were. He was Charlie Sheen in basketball shorts. Maybe that's a little extreme, but when you're dating and someone turns out to be a serial texter, it boosts your ego to chalk up their behavior to the fact that they're probably a sociopath. Maybe The Sequoia took another girl to the class and she levitated during the third-eye breathing exercise and he fell in love. I'll never know, but that was the last time I'd let a guy's rock-solid torso bewitch me into jumping up and down to the sounds of a didgeridoo.

Maybe now you can understand why I'm a little skeptical when it comes to spiritual experiences that require a financial transaction. It's probably better to rattle on endlessly with your friends until you feel better, or start a Happiness Improvement

Project with them, where you pull each other out of your collective and/or individual funks by going hiking, watching silly movies,[14] or jumping up and down to your favorite band until your brain is rattled and your spirit soars. And if you find that paying a man in lace bellbottoms to help you breathe through your third eye does help center you, then that's great. Just do it for yourself and not for some Sequoia.

---

14. Here are a few suggestions: *A Fish Called Wanda*, *Bride of Chucky* (Seed of Chucky works too), *Pure Luck*, *Airplane!*, *Clash of the Titans* (the original), *Flash Gordon*, *Best in Show*, *Raising Arizona*, *Modern Romance*, and *Bridesmaids*.

37

HOW TO TURN YOUR "BEACH BUNGALOW" INTO A "FITNESS OASIS"

We've talked about the perks of being a renter and the ways to trick yourself into believing that your tiny apartment is a "pied- à-terre" or a "homestead." Now it's time to create your very own "fitness oasis." All you'll need are some four-pound dumbbells, a plastic Hula-Hoop, a towel, the ability to play DVDs, a massive amount of self-discipline, and a can-do attitude.

I know some people are too cool to work out. They scoff at the rest of us, patting themselves on the back as they say, "Lifting a beer up to my face and pouring it down my throat is my workout" or "I don't diet, I eat McDonald's and ice cream every day" as they show off their six-pack abs and ballerina arms. That's great for them, but most of us have to lunge our asses off to stay in shape, doing leg lifts so excruciating someone dubbed them "the pretzel." As far as Brokenomics exercise goes, there are plenty of free workouts like jogging, biking, Tai Chi in the park, or swimming—if you live near an ocean or pond or pool, any(one's) pool. But what if it's sleeting? What if it's so hot that people are dropping dead, even just watching TV and eating a snow cone in the comfort of their living rooms? What do you do then? Spend all your money on a state-of-the-art gym that you can't afford? Not exercise? I guess if it's too hot to work out you could stand outside and sweat for an hour, but you're not really toning anything and it's a little dangerous, so please don't do that. I'd rather you enroll in two hundred SoulCycle classes than keel over because of my fitness tips.

Not all gym memberships are so extravagant that they'll bankrupt you, but I've saved over $2,600 in four years by not having a (low-priced) gym membership, which is a fact that I'd like to present to the Nobel Committee. It's not a huge amount of money when you spread it over four years, but it is enough to pay for some vacations or pressed juices. It's also enough to make a tiny dent in my student-loan payments. Maybe not even a dent. More like a little nick or a chip.

My fitness secret in some ways goes against my core beliefs and morals, but whatever. My secret is Billy Blanks. He's the Tae Bo fitness guru who's made a ton of money off people like me who buy his DVDs so they can jump around in the comfort of their own homes instead of paying for a gym. In the DVDs that I have, his outfits can best be described as *The Flintstones* meets Studio 54, which is great because the endless entertainment of his ensemble helps me get through all those roundhouse kicks. The downside to this plan is, of course, mind-numbing boredom. The outfits are funny, but not funny enough to make you forget you're doing the exact same kicks you've been doing for the last two hundred days.

> *My fitness secret in some ways goes against my core beliefs and morals, but whatever. My secret is Billy Blanks.*

It still surprises me when friends make fun of my Billy Blanks fitness plan. Yes it's repetitive, but then you mix it up with a Pilates DVD or a jog and it's not so bad. I did get a little depressed when my friend Sam, who was visiting from New York, sat on my bed and grilled me about my lifestyle and fitness choices one day:

Sam: *So, you work from home?*

DG: *Yep.*

Sam: *And you sleep and eat in this room too?*

DG: *Yes.*

Sam: *And you work out in here?*

DG: *Well . . . yes?*

Sam: *So basically this is your whole world?*

DG: *No. I get out. Sometimes.*

When she put it like that it did seem a little sad, but that didn't stop me from popping in my Billy Blanks DVD the very next day, after gently kicking her out and telling her to go get coffee for an hour so I could have room to jump around and throw some uppercuts at my phantom opponent. That's another great thing about this type of workout. If you get a parking ticket from an ornery meter maid or your boss pisses you off, you can channel your anger and release all that negative energy by pretending that you're kickboxing their head. I'm not condoning violence, but I am condoning a little psychological release in the form of pretend violence.

Now, to make this type of fitness oasis work for you, you need to like where you live, have at least enough room to do a jumping jack, and be OK exercising alone, monotonously, over and over like a robot. You also need the self-motivation to spontaneously start Hula-Hooping while you're watching TV or lift your dumbbells on a Saturday night in between doing your hair, taking sips of wine, and getting ready to go out. I know what you're thinking: "She is so incredibly disciplined." Don't worry, I promise with a little effort and a positive outlook, you, too can master this technique.

Let's break down the supplies:

- 4-pound dumbbells (or heavier): $15
- Plastic Hula-Hoop: $20–$30

- Towel: $7
- Workout DVD: $9.88

Besides your clothes and shoes, you're pretty much set. You can also skip the DVD and find workout videos at the library or on YouTube, if you want to be really savvy. This program works for me, but I will throw in the occasional non-SoulCycle spin class or jog just to mix it up so I don't have a nervous breakdown. Maybe it sounds horrible to you, and that's perfectly fine. I'm not offended. It's just a workout regimen. It doesn't define me. Not really. Well, maybe just a little.

The point is you don't have to spend a ton of money on fitness hiring a trainer to the stars. If you can do that without worrying about the cost, then it would be great if you could share everything you're learning with your friends and spread the wealth. What I can spread at this moment in time is the gospel of Hula-Hooping, free weights, and Billy's *Get Celebrity Fit Cardio* routine. Maybe you call that a sad excuse for a gym, but I prefer to call it a "fitness oasis." It works, it's cheap, and there's no commute. You just have to have a high threshold for tedium. Other than that, I highly recommend it.

VI.

EDUCATION

Only the educated are free.
—Epictetus

The future ain't what it used to be.
—Yogi Berra

38

A MODERN WARRIOR'S GUIDE
TO GRAD SCHOOL

Here's how it starts: you've been obsessively checking your mailbox or in-box or both like a crazed stalker for months when it arrives: the Acceptance Letter. The shimmering, faraway pipe dream you've worked so hard for and dreamed so often about suddenly comes into sharp focus. They said YES. You're going to school, following your passion, furthering your education—because that's the path that will lead you to a career as a pediatrician or a CEO or, god help you, anything having to do with the arts.

When I read the words, *"We are pleased to inform you . . ."* I'm pretty sure I broke into a spontaneous jig by the mailbox outside my apartment. I say "pretty sure" because the moment was so overwhelming that it's now a little fuzzy, kind of like your first encounter with a glass of good champagne: light, bubbly, drunken, maybe a little irrational. I knew I would have to pay for grad school somehow, but in that moment, none of it mattered. I had achieved a dream. A yes. Who wants to think about a succubus like Sallie Mae at a time like that?

I know it's melodramatic to think of student loan companies like Sallie Mae as evil mutant cyborgs that eats their young, but sometimes it does feel that way. They have no emotions. They plunder and pillage your bank account. They haunt your dreams. One lesson I learned after grad school, though, when I was at the height of my personal anti–Sallie Mae campaign, is that you shouldn't confuse education with benevolence. It's a business, with the exception of a few colleges that are free and utilitarian and that offer classes in both cow-milking and Kierkegaard. I don't mean that all professors and faculty members are Gordon Gekko disguised in corduroy elbow-patch jackets. And I'm not saying that we should roll over and play dead and allow the student loan industry and the rising cost of tuition to keep ballooning. I am saying that the system of higher education is a business, and the sooner you're able to come to terms with that, the better off you'll be. Plus, if you accept the fact that it's a business and not a philanthropic festival of learning, you'll be able to answer the question "Should I go to grad school?" in a much more rational way.

Maybe you're a naturally logical person who is an expert at guessing how many jellybeans are in a jar or calculating exactly how much you'll owe after graduation before you even step foot on campus. When I got into grad school I was not like that. I was too busy dancing on the sidewalk because I just knew that, whatever the future held, it would be sunny. And I kept right on dancing all the way to orientation. When you get into school yourself, I strongly urge you to do a celebration dance—but then gather your thoughts, catch your breath, sit down, and calculate approximately how much money you'll need, and how much you'll owe. In fact, do it before you start your undergraduate education as well. It's a real buzzkill, but it's a necessary one.

> *When you get into school yourself, I strongly urge you to do a celebration dance—but then gather your thoughts, catch your breath, sit down, and calculate approximately how much money you'll need, and how much you'll owe.*

You'll want to take some time to figure out the math because you'll be better off when you're faced with the endless bureaucratic paperwork and indecipherable mumbo jumbo they toss at you when you first get your loans. The whirlwind of getting into school, figuring out classes, and processing the fact that you're about to disappear down an academic rabbit hole for two or more years all while fighting off the "holy shit what have I done" feeling doesn't leave a whole lot of brain space to crack the code of which loans won't come back to haunt you, and which loans will shadow you like a stealth ninja for the rest of your days—or at least for the next thirty years, if you pay them off in time. With interest. So take the time now to find out the actual price of those classes—expect a lot of hidden costs like "lab fees" and "we own your soul" taxes, etc.— including the cost of finding a place to live and uprooting your life.

Every single college should add a financial-planning class to the curriculum and make it a requirement for all undergraduates. It would be a hell of a lot more useful than intermediate algebra or finite mathematics. No disrespect to the math lovers out there.

In old movies, people who owe a debt are usually bad guys: gamblers, mafia dudes, lowlifes, or shady billionaires. Kind of like tattoos, debt used to indicate crime and seediness. No self-respecting person had any, but now it's all so normal. I have tattoos *and* debt, so if you tossed me back to the year 1930, I'd be living in a seedy motel with a surly pimp named Johnny Bazooka who called me Toots. I'd traipse around in a red silk slip smoking out of a cigarette holder and saying things like, "Johnny, I'm gonna get outta this two-bit town and really *be* somebody! But first, pass me the hooch!" The point is—it's too bad debt is so mainstream now.

If you're ready to take on debt for grad school and you're thinking that you don't need to bother calculating how much you'll owe because it's all going to be swell and everyone will be wowed by your diploma, I'll share a little story about a reality check I experienced soon after graduating. I'm not sharing this to scare you or bum you out or turn you against grad school. I'm sharing it so you'll know that you need to prepare yourself because ridiculous things like this could happen to you too. Think of it as a shield or some ammo for post–graduate school life.

First things first—my graduate degree is in film. How's that for rational? Soon after graduating I interviewed to be a development assistant at a film production company. You're basically an assistant to an executive, and you get to read scripts and watch movies in between making calls, scheduling meetings, and fetching berry-flavored gum for your boss. I was excited. It was the kind of job I thought I wanted: stability, health insurance, a swipey security card, and free, multicolored Post-it notes. The pay—like any non-executive-level job in film—was crap. Translation: it would have been good (but still not great) if I didn't have student loan payments. It wasn't the end of the world though, because it was a job in the field I'd actually gone into debt to pursue. These days, that's called *really fucking promising.* I hit it off with the woman who would soon become my boss (let's call her Bonnie), but a few days later she said the CEO wanted to meet me before she could bring me on. She and I got along like a house on fire so I was sure the interview with the CEO would be as smooth and swift as a towering inferno. Let's call him Stan.

I chatted it up with Bonnie while I waited to meet Stan. Bonnie and I had similar taste in movies, which had me very excited. Any job is great, but it's so much cooler to work for someone who's heard of Werner Herzog than for someone who thinks "The Rock" is an underrated thespian and wants to cast him in a 3-D film version of *Waiting for Godot.* This type of creative spark ignites in Hollywood all the time. In fact, I bet some development execs are sitting around a conference table in Burbank right this second exclaiming: "Let's remake *Hamlet* with Miley Cyrus as Ophelia and that guy from One Direction as Hamlet. And we can make it a musical!! I can see the poster right now." People in Hollywood are very big on "seeing the poster" in their heads. If they can envision the poster, they believe the film will make loads of money and win Oscars, since it's so easily marketable. It's not an exact science, obviously, but maybe now you can understand why so many terrible movies get made.

After talking to Bonnie for a while, I was finally invited into Stan's office and we did the usual "Hi, How are you" hokeypokey. He glanced at my résumé and asked about my background. I said I was from Texas; he smiled. I said I loved movies; he nodded. I said I had an MFA in film. He said . . . "What's an MFA?" Keep in mind this isn't a four-year-old goat herder in Mongolia—this is a forty-something CEO of a film company in Los Angeles, U.S.A. I scanned my brain for an appropriate reply and settled on sheer fact: "It's a Master of Fine Arts." He said, "Oh" and moved on. Stan was not impressed. And here I was thinking those three letters— MFA—were pretty fancy. They definitely cost enough to be considered fancy.

"What kinds of movies do you like?" Stan asked. It was a little disheartening, but I knew I'd live. I was at a job interview! "I loved *The Diving Bell and the Butterfly*. Oh, and *The Lives of Others*. That was a great film," I said. Ah, I was so naive and green then, thinking that the CEO of a production company wanted to hear about artsy foreign films. "Those are *indie* films," he spat back at me, pronouncing the word "indie" as if it were code for "Nazi snuff porn." I thought fast. "Oh, well I also really love Will Smith movies and *Transformers*." He relaxed visibly and I got the job.

Maybe my degree didn't cause Stan to bow at my feet and declare me a genius, and maybe it didn't get me the job. I like to think it got me in the door, though. Obviously if you graduate at the top of your class from Johns Hopkins, your degree will impress potential employers, but if you're studying something that doesn't necessarily demand a graduate degree (philosophy, women's studies, film, acting, watercoloring from the heart), you should know that your diploma is not going to give you an automatic "in." It can give you a boost (maybe), but employers will be looking at who you are, what your work experience is, and what you can offer their company. Like selling your eggs or sperm or choosing to raise a potted plant instead of a human infant, going to grad school is a personal decision. No one can tell you what's best, which is why you have to figure it out for yourself.

I can't hold your hand, but I'd like to help, so here are some questions to ask yourself that might help clarify whether it's the right path for you. Ask them out loud while you're staring at your reflection in a mirror for maximum effect:

1. Why do I want to go to grad school?

2. What will I get out of it that I can't get from real-world experience?

3. Am I prepared to face my loans like an adult and not call Sallie Mae a succubus? At least, not all the time?

4. If necessary, can I tolerate the idea of temporarily going back to waiting tables or babysitting after getting my master's degree?

5. Do I have a clear sense of how much money it will cost and how much I might realistically make after graduating?

6. Will I take sole responsibility for my decision and not beat myself up when my grace period is over and I start paying the piper?

7. Will I work my ass off, as much as necessary, until I reach my goals or die of old age, whichever comes first?

8. Have I talked to people who have graduated with the degree I want and asked them about job prospects, the possibility of making enough money to pay the loans back, and whether they're happy with their decision or stuck in a black void of self-pity and despondency?

9. Have I explored all grants and scholarships, whether they offer a full ride or $50 a semester?

10. Have I educated myself about the dangers of private loans?

You can also write down a "pro" and "con" list on a sheet of paper to help you figure out if grad school is a wise decision. What you cannot do is ask a loan provider or someone who works in the financial aid office for advice. They are not looking out for your best interests. Does a meth dealer tell a potential client, "You know, now that I understand your situation I have to say: you really need to walk around the corner and get your fix from Ricky. Less variable interest." No. And neither does Sallie Mae or any other lender. And don't be fooled—people in the financial aid office are there to stamp things and wait for the clock to strike five o'clock so they can go home. They're not there to figure out your loans for you. Figure it all out before you start classes, and not while you're in the midst of your studies.

Between frequent fantasies about meeting Angelina Jolie and having her hand me a check to pay off my loans (she's a humanitarian—it's not so far-fetched), and dreaming of traveling to Delaware and tossing a big duffel bag full of cash onto the Sallie Mae lawn, I live in the real world and pay my debt, month by month, dollar by dollar. It's not fun being in debt, and there have been times when I've questioned my decision, but I loved the experience and learned things that eventually, after many sleepless nights, paid off. I met driven, creative people, and most of us are in the same boat, so we're rooting for each other and helping each other move forward in our careers. It's harder to find that kind of bond at work or at a bus stop.

If you go into grad school with a plan, a rational sense of the financial implications, and the willingness to accept the fact that you might come across a few Stans along the way, you'll be better prepared for whatever lies ahead. And that's the thing—you don't know what lies ahead. There are no guarantees. Nothing will be handed to you just because you went to class and studied hard for a few years. You'll be handed your diploma, but that's about it. And just remember that you may feel cozy and safe inside the warm cocoon of academia, learning about Shakespeare or 1970s cinema or the history of textile design, but it's still a business, and businesses don't run on the barter system. They run on your money.

Being passive when it comes to figuring out grad school and student loans is like showing up to a duel armed with your dashing good looks and charming personality: you'll wind up sprawled out in the dirt and gushing blood (i.e., money), cursing the universe and wondering why you didn't plan ahead. Did the ancient Greeks head into battle buck naked, unarmed, and without a plan? They were fairly naked, but they did wear little pleated skirts, cute yet utilitarian gladiator sandals, fierce helmets, and armored tops. Did the Vikings shrug and leave their axes and swords on the ship when heading out to raid an enemy? Maybe occasionally when they were wasted, but they most certainly didn't make a habit of it. Would you try and satisfy a demon succubus's lust for money by handing it your diploma and saying, "Here, take my MFA"? No. If you decide to go into debt for grad school, you need to arm yourself with knowledge, a plan, and an understanding of variable interest rates, private loan repayment, consolidation, and the consequences of defaulting. You need to make a solemn vow not to blame outside forces for your decision—unless someone actually hogtied you, enrolled you in school, and forced you to take out loans against your will. And, finally, if you've done the homework and decided that grad school is for you, you need to make "No Regrets" your battle cry.

And then you need to work your ass off and try and enjoy the ride, even if you are paying a hefty toll to a mutant cyborg each month, with interest.

39

SO YOU WANT TO MAJOR
IN PHILOSOPHY

As a kid, my idea of the perfect profession bounced between archeologist, writer, dream doctor (that lucrative field where you wear a lab coat and analyze people's dreams), and stripper. In sixth grade my friends and I were obsessed with Mötley Crüe and the "Girls, Girls, Girls" video and we thought that moving to Hollywood and grinding against metal poles on the Sunset Strip would be a romantic way to find and marry someone in the band. How could they resist us in our baggy T-shirts, wind shorts, and Keds? My friend Kari was destined to marry Tommy Lee, Erin set her sights on Nikki Sixx, and I had my wedding to Vince Neil all planned out. No one had claimed Mick Mars because we were a bunch of superficial preteens and didn't yet have the life experience to realize that Mick was probably the real catch. We were too enamored of their big hair, handsome faces, and pink lipstick to pay much attention to Mick. Sorry, dude.

By high school, the gleam of the stripper pole had dulled and we graduated from Mötley Crüe to Morrissey. Sophomore year I refocused my career goals and decided that I wanted to be an animal-rights activist. Encouraged by an English teacher I adored for her progressively spiky hair and passion for E.E. Cummings, I joined her group A.C.T. (Animals Count Too), threw out all my lotions and products containing horse hooves and whale sperm, stopped eating meat, and—to the horror of my carnivorous family—marched outside Texas gun and game shows hoisting signs reading, IVORY IS FOR BEASTS! and MEAT IS MURDER! I pledged that I would find a way to make a living at this, somehow. How could it not work out, with all that passion brewing inside me? For better or worse, more practical trades like dentist, accountant, or computer scientist never entered my mind. A life of such left-brained, math-intensive pursuits would have caused my histrionic soul to curl up, roly-poly style, and die.

Plenty of people make the decision to play guitar for fun instead of trying to be the next Jack White or Joan Jett. These people major in business or become surgeons. They get health insurance and make enough to hit up a Sandals resort a few times a year. On the weekends, they grab their ax and jam in their garage out in Poughkeepsie with their neighbor Marvin who works in the IT department and loves kolaches. They might say, "Dude, I could have been the next Hendrix . . . installing routers just isn't my passion." But, then again, their loans are paid off, and they're not insurance-less has-beens, saddled with music school debt, rolling around in a ditch somewhere, cuddling a stolen bottle of Cold Duck and mumbling, "I should have majored in computer science!"

There are no guarantees in life, of course. Lots of über-wealthy people wind up rolling around in (fancy, metaphorical) ditches for whatever reason. Following your passion is important, but if your dream is indeed dreamy, you need to balance that with a career reality check here and there. Say philosophy sets your soul on fire. Before you blindly race toward your degree, reach out to people who majored in philosophy. Find out how you can make money and what your options will be after you're abruptly ejected from the safety of the classroom into the cold, hard world where people are more interested in Katy Perry than Jacques Derrida. And don't just hit up the world's most successful living philosophy majors, like

Ricky Gervais—that's cheating. Does a job teaching philosophy at a community college in Nebraska or Delaware sound fulfilling to you? Are you prepared to fight your way into a paying career, even if it takes a few (or several) years? Do you love philosophy so much that any ups and downs along the way will be worth it, since you're pursuing your life's passion? Do you want to study philosophy and then go to law school? If you answered yes to any of these questions, then by all means, go get your Heidegger on.

A philosophy or poetry degree is an easy target for ridicule. The more cold-hearted members of our society look down on these professions, which is a shame. I admit that I have, on occasion, when I've felt ridiculous for getting degrees in english and film, thought, "Well at least I didn't major in poetry." That's a really jerky thought, but if you do decide to go after a "risky" career, you might occasionally need to build yourself up by ridiculing someone else's choice of major. Just do it silently, so no one knows.

If you do choose to major in something dreamy, you'll need to stockpile an arsenal of coping mechanisms. All of those articles like "The 10 Majors that Will Ruin Your Life" or "Top 10 Degrees that Intelligent People Pursue so They Won't Be Broke Losers" are not fun to read if you did choose philosophy or painting or poetry over computer science, engineering, or finance. Still, the world would be full of automatons if no one took a chance and everyone chose to stifle their passion in the pursuit of money for money's sake. If money is your passion, and that's what drives you to study finance, then that's your choice. Just be sure you share your fancy clothes with your college buddies once you graduate and land that sweet corner office. Give back to the community—the community being your right-brained, overeducated, underemployed friends.

At a certain point in life the glamorous stereotype of the starving artist doesn't seem so glam. Maybe that's because of the Internet, and because of all those aforementioned articles telling us that certain majors, which once seemed so pleasant, will leave us destitute, while the information systems majors are all partying with six-foot-tall models on Paul Allen's yacht. If pursuing your dream to the bitter end and majoring in something from one of the "10 Majors that Will Ruin Your Life" lists is more appealing to you than having threesomes on yachts during your lunch break, here are a few tips that might help you get through the dark, dark times, when you're curled into a ball in the corner of your room, cursing Simone de Beauvoir or Walt Whitman:

1. Crush your own ego. If you've decided to major in a subject that's more cerebral and artistic and less practical or fiscally responsible, you need to annihilate your ego. Tell it who's boss. Crush it before everyone else starts to. You will face rejection, humiliation, and setbacks. You will fetch berry-flavored gum for a boss along the way because you need a paycheck. You need to be prepared for these things, and the first step is to remember that you are not above it. You are in it. At least until you've worked hard enough to break out of it. And even then, you could find yourself back in it when you least expect it because life's a bitch. That's pretty much Philosophy 101.

2. Build your ego into an indestructible force of nature. Once you've pummeled your self-esteem, you need to help it rise from the ashes, like a phoenix from the flames, or like Iron Man in his suit. No one can ever stop you. You are destined to set the world on fire. If you can achieve a healthy balance between number one and number two on this list, you're on your way to greatness. Or at least on your way to survival. Survival is probably more realistic.

3. Roll with the punches. *Cool Hand Luke*, one of the best films ever made, stars Paul Newman as Luke, a rebellious hero who gets sentenced to a chain gang for cutting the heads off parking meters. He makes some of the other prisoners jealous and uncomfortable because he's quiet and doesn't partake in their chain gang shenanigans. He's an iconoclast. There's a classic scene where Luke is challenged to a boxing match with his archrival, Dragline. Luke's getting beaten to a pulp, to the point where the other prisoners start averting their eyes and begging him to just stay down. Even Dragline finally tells him to stay down. But Luke does not stay down. He pulls himself up off the dirt, over and over, until it becomes excruciating to watch, and he tells Dragline "You're gonna hafta kill me." If you major in something iffy, you better make that your motto, and make Luke your patron saint. Just keep getting up, even if it feels like your teeth have been knocked out and your eyes are crossed from the blows that life is dealing you.

4. Punch obstacles in the face. Now it's time to talk offense. You've mastered the art of rolling with the punches, so now you need to learn when to punch back and push through. You'll probably have to do this a lot, mentally. Maybe physically, too. Don't punch people, but punching the air while kickboxing (please refer back to chapter 37), throwing a right hook at a pillow, or pounding your fist on a chair or table are perfectly healthy ways to cope. Pound your fist hard enough to make yourself feel better, but not so hard that you injure yourself. Find a happy medium. You might find yourself in this position after a layoff, when you don't get a raise you asked for, when you get the fifth rejection letter from the documentary film fund you have your heart set on, or when the grad school of your dreams puts you on a waitlist. Don't let any of these things stop you. Punch a pillow and forge ahead.

5. Envision your deathbed. Remember back in chapter 23 (Couch Potato Today, Gone Tomorrow) how I urged you to go travel because if you didn't you'd be on your deathbed full of regrets? Well, that scare tactic can apply to majors as well. Imagine yourself at the end of it all, as your life flashes before your eyes and you're remembering your first-grade crush, the birth of your child, and the pastrami sandwich you ate on March 16, 2010. Would you be OK thinking back on your choice of major? Would it fill you with pride, dread, or regret? If you cannot fathom not pursuing your dream major no matter what the cost, then maybe that's a sign. If you think you'd rather have your dying thought be, "I loved archeology but I'm so happy I'm in a California King–sized bed and not a cot right now due to the fact that I chose engineering and tinkered with archeology on the side," then that's a sign too. Heed them.

And just remember, Luke was the hero of the movie even though he was a rebellious "original." He just had to withstand a serious beating and a ton of ridicule, and he had to stand his ground, even when his face was in the dirt. I won't spoil the ending for you, but the last scene isn't Luke partying on a yacht with a bunch of Victoria's Secret models. If you want that ending for yourself, you probably do need to focus on a more practical field and philosophize and read poetry on your downtime, to relax.

40

DENIAL, ANGER, BARGAINING, DEPRESSION, ACCEPTANCE, DIRECT DEPOSIT

L ike the adorable names Fanny Mae and Freddie Mac, Sallie Mae sounds like a cute, apron-wearing, cherry-pie-baking character from *Hee Haw* or *The Beverly Hillbillies* instead of a vile, soulless demon puppet. One day, just for fun, and because I wanted to see if I was the only one who anthropomorphized my student loan lender by referring to "her" as a fanged goblin or a two-headed banshee, I played a little Sallie Mae word-association game with some grad school friends. Here are the results of my research:

- CONFUSING!
- Bastards
- Diabolical
- Interest
- Shit
- Slave

- Deceit
- Omnipresent
- A Racket
- Wicked Witch of the East
- BROKE!
- Suicide

- Devil
- The Man
- Injustice

- Trapped
- Debt forever
- Hell

Not a "sweet little old lady" in sight. They really should just name it Student Loan Corp or Vortex Inc. or something—call it what it is. The cutesy name is like throwing salt in the wound. I wouldn't be surprised if a new *Friday the 13th* horror franchise pops up in the next few years with a demented psycho killer called Sallie Mae who looks like a cross between Freddy Krueger, Pinhead from *Hellraiser*, and Medusa. Of course, this is a very immature way to talk about student loans, but sometimes you just need a release, and calling corporations mean names has a way of making you feel better.

If you did get out of school without calculating how much you would owe, and if you find yourself in the midst of a meltdown because you cannot figure out how you're going to pay back all that money, you might be tempted to call 1-888-2-SALLIE, push some buttons until you get a customer service person, and scream, "Why is this happening?" or "Why can't you save me?!" I understand how you feel—it's an unhealthy emotional cocktail made up of rage, helplessness, and guilt. Unfortunately that doesn't mean you can scream at people.

After graduation you learn pretty quickly that calling Sallie Mae for help is about as fruitful as asking a Pfizer rep to recommend some herbal remedies. Don't expect them to save you. That's your job. They're not your mommy. They're not paid enough to hold your hand, wipe your tears, and sing you a lullaby until the nightmare goes away. They're there to . . . answer the phone, basically.

I admit I did get a little testy with a Sallie Mae customer service person once or twice, just like I've gotten testy with a Time Warner Cable rep about, I'd say, forty times. And I will say that when I went a little berserk after calling 1-888-2-SALLIE it was a scary time in my life: I didn't have a job, I'd just gone through a terrible breakup, I was broke, and I had a pile of debt looming over me. So I called Sallie Mae, hoping they would help me. Looking back, it's probably one of the most naïve things I've ever done—and I've done a lot of stupid things. I hope the customer service person flipped off his headset when I said, "Can't you help me? I'm screwed!?" because I really deserved it, even if I was vulnerable, lost, and temporarily staying at my parents' house in Texas and taking my mom's Lunesta when I made the call.

Unless a customer service person is truly being a douchebag, it's not fair to get angry with them. It's not their fault. They're getting paid to listen to jerks like us complain all day. They don't run the companies or use our money to charter private jets. They probably go home after work, pop in a TV dinner, watch *Wheel of Fortune*, and tell their loved ones about all the crybabies they had to deal with that day.

If you really want to change the student loan system, do it in a productive way. Get involved with organizations and politicians who are trying to revamp the system. No matter how frustrated and scared you are about your student loans, do not take it out on the wrong person: the customer service person, the grocery bagger, your podiatrist, the UPS guy. It might seem wise in the heat of the moment, but it will not make your loans go away. Neither will staying calm and addressing these people politely, but at least you won't have some stranger in a cubicle flipping you off, and at least you won't be ruining someone else's day.

You will likely experience an anarchic typhoon of emotions when you graduate and realize that all that money you borrowed for school needs to be paid back. To help you through that time and make you feel less alone, here is a rundown of the emotional states you'll likely experience along the way:

> **Denial.** *Debt? What debt? I didn't spend the last few years paying to sit and listen to lectures on free will and Samoan marriage rituals; I was climbing my way up the corporate ladder and getting paid. I am not in debt. I am* rich. Physical symptoms during this stage may include a feeling of euphoria followed by a hunch

that something is amiss, followed again by euphoria in a repetitive cycle on and on until . . .

Anger. *The entity that let me take out all those student loans without doing a credit check or counseling me on the idiocy of taking out private loans is a succubus/demon/troll/fanged goblin/criminal/malignant fiend.* Symptoms of anger may include: screaming at customer service people, stabbing your student loan bill with a kitchen knife, drinking, banging your head against concrete walls, Googling the CEO of your student loan lender to see how much they make per year.[15]

Bargaining. *Dear Universe (or whoever), please make it so that my lender gets caught in a giant fraud scandal, which causes the president of the United States and every human being on the planet to unanimously agree that the proper and just punishment will be to shut down the company and make all of our loans disappear. If you make this happen, I'll give you my firstborn child, a bouquet of roses, or some macaroons. Whatever you want.* Symptoms of bargaining: an imagination running amok.

Depression. *I'll just lie here on my back, staring at the ceiling, trying to suffocate myself with my diploma.* Symptoms of depression include: depression.

Acceptance. *This whole suffocation-by-diploma plan isn't working, so I may as well get up, take a shower, acknowledge that I owe a large sum of money but it's because I decided to invest in myself and in my future and go after a career that I'm passionate about. I will make this work. Somehow.* Symptoms of acceptance include: the will to live and a slight puffing of the chest.

---

15. I strongly advise you not to do this. Ever. I did and the number was so outrageous it sent me into a tailspin of alternating rage and ennui, which I still haven't fully recovered from.

Direct deposit. *I am finally able to pay at least the minimum amount each month, so I will set up a direct deposit, since it will lower my interest rate an infinitesimal yet meaningful amount and, best of all, I will not have to be reminded of the succubus each month since the money will be pried out of my account and into the lender's cold, withered claws without me having to write a check and waste even more money putting a stamp on the bill.* Symptoms of direct deposit include: a healthy infusion of stoicism.

Once classes end and your grace period is over, you may find yourself moving through these very common Post-Graduation Stages of Despair (PGSD). Don't avoid them. Feel your feelings. In so doing, you will be able to blossom from a despondent fool into a hopeful (or at least semi-hopeful) member of society. And then the real work begins.

VII.

WORK

You can do anything you set your mind to.
—Loads of parents

You can't fire me—you don't even know my name!
—Margaret Burre, *Clockwatchers*

41

HOW TO BABYSIT AND
NOT HAVE A BREAKDOWN

Bad things happen to babysitters. Murderous strangers call them on the landline and say passive-aggressive things like, "Have you checked the children?" They're stalked by knife-wielding psycho killers like Michael Myers. And, most terrifying of all, they're subject to ridicule, crippling self-doubt, and debilitating, angst-ridden thoughts about the direction their career has taken and the realization that they could be watching *Yo Gabba Gabba* reruns for the rest of their working lives. If you've seen the show, you know that's a horrifying prospect.

Before college or grad school, when you're in junior high or high school, being a babysitter is cool. You have status and rank. You're lording over littler kids, drinking as many Cokes as you want, and ruling the roost. You're the boss. The CEO. The tyrant-in-charge. That all changes at a certain age, like after you've worked hard and tried to land your dream job only to find that positions are scarce and you need a paycheck. It's even worse when you're over thirty and you find yourself babysitting a friend's toddler after a layoff, which is what happened to me. If nannying is your career, that's a different story. I'm talking about accidental, last-resort babysitting. The kind where you have health benefits and a paycheck one minute, and a constant cold and an inconsistent cash flow the next.

I babysat in high school and college, but I didn't really expect to return to that position after landing a "stable" post–grad school job. As I searched for work after my layoff, I was engaged in a glorious trifecta of babysitting, cat-sitting, and plant-sitting, in between getting unemployment checks when I needed them. One day, a very good friend of mine, who happens to be a world-class sharer of clothes, asked if I wanted to babysit her son three days a week since her regular babysitter was leaving. I liked her son (code name: Baby B), the money was good, and I was in no position to decline her very generous offer. It wasn't glamorous, but money is money, and I needed some. So there I was, strolling Baby B around Santa Monica, changing his diapers, wishing I had a T-shirt that said I'M JUST THE BABYSITTER every time we passed a hot guy, weathering his tantrums when the chocolate stopped working, and wondering what the hell happened to my life.

One day at work when Baby B and I were deep in conversation about whether Nemo the fish ate raisins, he peered up at me with a strange glint in his eye and commanded: "Dina CRY!" As I emphasized before, I love kids, so at first it was cute. I humored him by contorting my face into my best meltdown impression, and I rubbed my eyes with balled-up fists, mime-crying, "Whaaaa!" over and over. He loved it. We giggled. I figured it was done. "Dina CRY! CRY Dina!" Suddenly the strange glint in his eyes took on a much more sinister tone, and an ancient survival instinct welled up inside me.

"No more crying," I said as calmly as I could. "I want to be happy now!" He frowned and crinkled his little brow. "Dina CRY." Maybe I was a thirty-something laid-off babysitter with student loans, no boyfriend, and no health insurance, but I sure as hell did not want to cry in front of this little kid. I wanted to cry in my apartment, with vodka. "CRY!" He was actually starting to make me feel a little despondent. "Let's have some chocolate!" I said in a chipper voice so phony it would make Holden Caulfield spontaneously combust. That did the trick, for the kid at least. He shrugged off the sadism and ate his chocolate. I know it's bad to bribe children with candy, but it's better than the babysitter having a breakdown.

That was kind of a low point for me, career-wise. Not the babysitting so much as the emotional abuse at the hands of a living Chucky doll. But life goes on! I triumphed (with the help of some M&M's) and resolved to get out of the babysitting racket for good.

In an ideal world you graduate from college, create a glowing résumé, and land a stable, well-paying gig within months. We all know that doesn't always happen. Sometimes it takes a while to land a job, sometimes you get laid-off, and sometimes you need to step away from the nine-to-five to focus on your start-up or figure out what you really want out of life. Babysitting is a great way to discover that you don't want to babysit. It has that perk going for it.

If you do find yourself babysitting during a time in life when you thought you'd be somewhere else career-wise, there are ways to survive and even appreciate the fact that you're dealing with snot and baby wipes instead of expense accounts and promotions. First, try and think of it as your "babysitting interlude" rather than your "career slump that defines who you are and what you're about." An interlude is short and temporary, and it even rings of escape, as if babysitting is just a mini career "vacation" until the next fabulous leg of the journey. It can be your time to figure things out. Let it motivate you. Every time the kid you're babysitting screeches or commands you to "CRY!" you should take all that pent-up frustration and try and turn it into something positive, like fierce determination to get the hell out and get a different job as soon as humanly possible. The baby's naptime is when you should be rewriting your five-year plan.

Another trick is to remember that this interlude is teaching you an incredibly important skill, and that skill is superhuman resilience, which is necessary in any career. Surviving more than an hour with an infant or a toddler whose only goal in life is to manipulate you, reduce you to tears, and psychologically beat you into submission is like boot camp for the corporate world. If you can get through a babysitting session emotionally unscathed, you have learned skills no professor could teach you. Babysitting also helps you develop patience and prepares you to stand up for yourself in the face of oppression. Telling Baby B that I was finished crying was a big step for me. I didn't let him walk all over me. I stood up for myself in the face of a two-year-old. That's a learned skill that has been very useful when dealing with both kids and adults.

Finally, in addition to bolstering your resilience, patience, and guts, babysitting will also remind you about that all-important Brokenomics Rule #9: Why have a baby when you can just get a nice potted plant? If you do decide on the baby and not the plant, babysitting will help you enter parenthood with

> *Surviving more than an hour with an infant or a toddler whose only goal in life is to manipulate you, reduce you to tears, and psychologically beat you into submission is like boot camp for the corporate world.*

a solid understanding of what you're in for. Times ten thousand.

I hope you don't wind up babysitting in your thirties after a layoff. I hope your career path is as smooth and swift and upwardly mobile as a rocket ship. If, by some chance, it isn't, remember that setbacks are interludes, as long as you face them with determination, a plan, and the ability to pull yourself out of them. Babysitting (or waitressing or barista-ing) happens—endure it gracefully, with grit, until the next stage of your career emerges. There's nothing shameful about post-grad babysitting. At least you're working, and that's something to be proud of. You got out of bed, put on clothes, and earned some money, just like Donald Trump or Sheryl Sandberg, but the babysitter version. It's an interlude—and, like any career, it doesn't define you unless you let it.

42

A TOUGH-LOVE GUIDE TO
INTERNSHIPS

Beware: you are about to enter one of those "I used to walk fifty miles in the snow to school" rants, but when it's all over, in approximately five pages, you'll emerge with a renewed faith in humanity and a fierce drive to succeed. You'll be a better person. Either that or you'll still be exactly the same as you are right this second, which is fine too.

Let's begin.

Back in my day (stay with me here), unpaid internships were a given. In the entertainment industry, which is the ridiculous, wonderful, idiotic industry that I chose, everyone took on unpaid internships. It was a way to get your foot in the door, build a résumé, and network during college so you could hopefully get a paying job after graduating. We never confused "internship" with "job." That's both a good and a bad thing.

People should get paid for their work. If a company is having you come in forty hours a week and they're paying you nothing—you need to leave. In an ideal world, all internships would be paid, but the world is shifty and unfair, so many internships pay in experience and free coffee. If a giant corporation or movie studio can afford to pay interns a little something, they should. Smaller companies often can't do that, but they need the help, and to compensate for your work they can—and should—take time to mentor you and make it worthwhile for you to photocopy their papers and answer their calls for free. Maybe it's bad that we suffered through our two- or three-day-a-week internships without suing or protesting and asking for pay. Maybe we were wimps. I don't think so though.

I've been on both sides of the internship divide. I've been the lowly intern (many times), and I've been the person who hired the interns. The latter position is much better, obviously, but I didn't get there by leaping straight from college into a fancy job where I could boss people around and make myself feel superior by tormenting them. I didn't torment people because I knew what it was like to be an intern, and because I'm not a tyrant. I should probably be a tiny bit more tyrannical, but when you're raised by a Southern mother who constantly warns, "Don't be a Hateful Hannah!" during your formative years, it's not so easy to channel your inner Nero. I tried reading Sun Tzu's *The Art of War* when I was angling for a promotion at the job that eventually laid me off, but I got through three chapters and realized I didn't want to become a cold-hearted, calculating, ancient Chinese military general in order to get ahead. I did get a raise and a promotion, but then I got laid-off, so maybe I should have finished the book.

That was the job that put me in charge of hiring the interns, which was an eye-opening experience. Some of the interns were hardworking and conscientious, and others were perpetually late, flakey, and calculating—maybe the calculating ones had read Sun Tzu. The wiliest intern I dealt with was not named Bane,[16] but that's the name I'm giving him and you'll soon see why. Bane had a great résumé and an upbeat attitude, and he knew a lot about comic books, which, this being Hollywood 2009, was reason enough to bring him on. The first few weeks were great, but then he turned— and his dark, duplicitous nature emerged.

---

16. The Batman villain who inhaled a venomous super steroid through his facemask.

"Can you make two copies of this script for me?" I asked Bane one day. This was a totally reasonable request. He'd copied scripts before, I'd copied scripts before—interns copied scripts. Bane folded his arms across his chest, which was covered by a faded *X-Men* T-shirt. He'd quickly gone from dressing like he cared to dressing like a guy who wore faded comic book T-shirts to his internship.

"It's not my job to copy scripts," Bane shot back. If I had finished reading *The Art of War,* I probably would have beheaded him or at least publicly shamed him in some barbaric way, but instead I stared at him, thinking of a response. And then, like a bolt of lightning, one came to me.

"Yeah, it is," I said. Bane took the script, pouted all the way to the Xerox machine, and made the copies. A few days later, I was sitting in the conference room with Bane and two other interns, because I was trying to be some sort of mentor and make the unpaid internship worth their while by answering questions and listening to ideas during lunch. "I'm never going to be someone's assistant," Bane declared. And then, for a brief second, it sounded like he was speaking through a cage-like, venomous mouthpiece when he said, "I want to run shit."

We'd all like to "run shit" and not have to obey a boss, but unless you're staging a coup or you have millions of dollars and can just start a company and call yourself the CEO, you have to pay your dues and work your way up. Bane obviously had other plans.

"So, what do you want to do?" I asked.

"I told you. I want to run shit." This could possibly have been admirable if Bane had sat up straight and followed his statement with something like, "And I'm prepared to work hard and learn and put in the time to get there." He didn't though. He pouted, slouched in the chair, and ate a curly fry. Even though he knew a lot about comic books, Bane didn't last much longer as an intern. His attitude got worse, he'd show up late, and he definitely didn't act like a guy who was on his way to running anything, unless it was a bitching session at a Whiny Entitled Babies Anonymous meeting.

Way back in chapter 3 (Be Your Own Life Coach) I advised

you to never assume. Bane assumed a lot—he assumed the world owed him, he assumed he deserved to run shit, and he assumed he wouldn't get fired from an unpaid internship. Just because you think you deserve something does not mean you deserve it. You deserve things when you work your ass off. At least, that's my philosophy.

If internships are a necessary stepping-stone in your chosen career, think of them as just that: a stepping-stone. Now that you've cleared that hurdle, here are a few quick tips to help you tolerate, survive, and maybe even excel at whatever internship you take on:

Timing is everything. Marilyn Monroe was always late, so her acting teacher, the famous Lee Strasberg, told her, that if she couldn't be on time, she should just be early.[17] If you're interviewing for an internship, don't be late. Don't think of it as "just an internship." And don't be late once you get it either. If you are late, call or email. Treat it like a job and be on time. This is crucial if you want to try and impress the bosses and get hired or get a good reference. Otherwise, why are you even there?

Suck it up. No one likes copying or filing or taking coffee orders. If you're an intern this shouldn't be all that you're doing, but it is something you'll get asked to do. Don't assume you're above it.

Choose your battles. If you're interning and someone asks you to work a twelve-hour day and also go buy their mistress some lingerie, that's a battle worth fighting. If they ask you to make copies or answer a call, that's not.

Network. The whole idea of networking and schmoozing is pretty gross, but in most careers it's a necessary evil. It doesn't have to be a horrible experience if you approach it like a normal, laid-back human being rather than an uptight, grinning sycophant. As an intern, don't be afraid to ask the bosses and

---

17. "He Befriended Monroe, He Scolds Pacino, He Makes Burstyn Cry: It's Lee Strasberg of the Method" People December 1976, by Mary Vespa http://www.people.com/people/archive/article/0,,20067218,00.html

the assistants to coffee or lunch. They may say no (if they're jerks), but chances are they'll say yes and you can soak up their wisdom, request their advice, and show them that even though you're mainly copying and answering phones, you care, and you're someone they should remember.

Have a paying job. There's a reason that internships are not called jobs. During college, most everyone I knew had a paying job plus an internship. Do your internship two or three days a week, for a few hours, and then have your regular job. Don't take an internship that doesn't allow you to work if you need to.

Have a sense of humor. As with all things—relationships, life, money, politics—internships are so much more tolerable if you have a sense of humor. Don't laugh it off if they're treating you horribly or doing illegal things like making you work full-time with no breaks for free, but don't be a scowling pouter like Bane. I don't know where he is now, but I doubt he's running shit. The most successful people know when to laugh it off. Except maybe military generals and prison wardens. Those jobs probably require an absence of humor, at least while you're on duty.

And that concludes my "I walked fifty miles in the snow" sermon. I wish for you only paid internships, fabulous career advances, and the ability to run shit without experiencing too much humiliation along the way. If it's not all smooth sailing and you find an unpaid internship that will actually be good for your career and that's worth doing, then do it well, suck it up, read *The Art of War* if you have to—but please, whatever you do, don't be a Bane.

43

HOW TO SURVIVE A LAYOFF

t happened on a Tuesday. I know this because you never forget the day they laid you off. It's burned into your brain, like a psychic battle scar, or a brand on a cow's ass. My brand reads: TUESDAY, MARCH 16, 2010, AT APPROXIMATELY 9:00 AM ON A SUNNY DAY IN LOS ANGELES, FIFTEEN FLOORS UP.

A handful of friends and coworkers had been laid-off at my company over the previous eighteen months (including Bane, the fiendish intern), but I felt that my position inside this particular cubicle was pretty secure. I'd just gotten a raise a few months before, and no one got laid-off after getting a pay raise. That would just be ludicrous. Laughable, even. A real knee-slapper. But this was 2010, the year that redheaded Jet Blue flight attendant grabbed a beer and cruised down the emergency slide because he was mad as hell and he wasn't going to take it anymore (either that or he was just a crackpot angling for a reality-show contract). It was the year Snooki was arrested for disorderly conduct on *Jersey Shore*, and Miley Cyrus won Favorite Breakout Movie Actress at the People's Choice Awards. The world was fucked, and no one was safe. Except maybe Snooki. Her novel, *A Shore Thing*, was published the very next year and became a best seller.

Layoffs have a way of turning your life upside down and making you a little upside down and crazy in the head as well. Case in point: I actually checked *A Shore Thing* out of the Santa Monica library when it came out and read it cover to cover. Well, more like cover (skip some pages about spray tanning) to cover.[18] I had become a little infatuated with Nicole "Snooki" Polizzi since my layoff, and I thought of her as some sort of celebrity totem or spirit animal—but a spirit animal with a pouf. I didn't try and copy her hairdo or anything, but I admired her attitude and spunk. I needed it. I found inspiration in Vince Lombardi's wisdom too, but Snooki was my mini burnt orange Buddha. If you're scoffing right this second, take a moment and meditate on this:

> I don't care what people think about me. If you like it, we're friends. If you don't, you're my enemy; peace out. That's how everybody should be, otherwise you're going to be depressed all the time.[19]

Snooki said that in *Rolling Stone*, and I did and still do find it to be a very inspirational quote. It's especially uplifting when you're unemployed and feeling depressed all the time. "Peace out" was right. I may have been laid-off, but that didn't mean I couldn't conquer the world. Somehow. Someday. As soon as I got a job. Snooki's wisdom was helping me reclaim my sense of self-worth and my pride, and I'm not ashamed of that. Some people turn to Pema Chödrön in times of crisis. I turned to Snooki. Whatev, bitches!

There are hundreds of thousands of layoff stories out there, unfortunately. Mine didn't literally happen at 9:00 AM, but that's when it all began, for me at least. My boss and the CEO and the accountant knew it was happening before then, obviously, but I came into work that day just like I had done all the days before for the last two years, with an Earl Grey tea and a gooey Morning Glory Muffin from The Coffee Bean downstairs. I settled in and started

---

18. There was high demand for the novel, so I had to put my name on a waitlist.
19. "The Wild, The Stupid & The Jersey Shore Shuffle" *Rolling Stone* August 2010, by Jenny Eliscu http://www.rollingstone.com/culture/news/the-wild-the-stupid-the-jersey-shore-shuffle-rolling-stones-2010-feature-20110222

checking my email, and then it happened: an instant message popped up on my screen. It was from my boss (who was sitting five feet away from me, FYI), and it read: CAN YOU MEET FOR BREAKFAST TOMORROW MORNING AT 8:30 AT BLUE PLATE ON MONTANA? This might sound like a fabulous invitation to you, but the second I read it I felt flushed and nauseous, and I just knew. It was a bright sunny day, and I was about to be laid-off.

Call me paranoid if you must, but in the two years we had worked together my boss and I had never gone to breakfast. We'd had lunch, coffee, and closed-door meetings in her office if we needed to discuss anything. Breakfast? Never. Maybe I have potential as a Sherlock because I wasn't fooled for a second. Blue Plate is delicious, and Montana Avenue is very swanky, but she wasn't inviting me to a blueberry pancake breakfast to tell me how wonderful she thought I was. She was inviting me so she could kick me to the curb in what she thought would be a nice, respectful way. I appreciate that now, but at the time it kind of made me want to puke.

There was no way I was waiting around in the dark (or beneath a bunch of fluorescent lights) for twenty-four hours to get the news. I didn't need a free meal that bad—yet. I contemplated writing her back, and then quickly started typing, CAN WE TALK? Before I could hit SEND I saw her walk out of her office and disappear into the conference room for a meeting. Suddenly, the urge to know the truth became dire. I checked her schedule and saw that she had back-to-back meetings all day. I couldn't just sit in my cubicle in anticipation all day long, and I definitely didn't have the stomach or the motivation to do any work, so I grabbed my phone and my wallet and headed outside for some air.

As soon as I walked out of the building, I dialed my dad in Texas to get his opinion about my boss's Blue Plate scheme. He's the perfect person to call in times of crisis because he stays calm and cool, and he always says just the right thing to make you feel a little better. As soon as he picked up I blurted, "Dad? I think they're laying me off."

"What? Well, why do you think that? Did they tell you?"

"No, but my boss invited me to breakfast at eight-thirty tomorrow morning. We've never gone to breakfast."

As soon as I said it, I felt a little silly. Maybe I was being paranoid. Breakfast is harmless. Pancakes symbolize positivity and joy in some cultures. Why would my boss spend money on me just to lay me off? I waited for my dad to make all the paranoia and doubt go away, since that was one of his fatherly duties.

"So, what do you think?" I asked hopefully.

"Shit."

"What?"

"Shit, honey."

That wasn't really the response I was expecting or hoping for. How about, "You're being silly," or "Go back to work, everything is fine, she probably wants to tell you she's doubling your salary." Instead, I got, "Shit, honey."

And he was right. The second my boss came back from her last meeting of the day, at 3:00 PM—talk about an agonizing six hours—I hurried to her office door and blurted, "Can we talk?" And, behind closed doors, we did. And I got laid-off. And we never went to that pancake breakfast. We parted on good terms, and most everyone I knew at that job ended up leaving or getting laid-off eventually, and they're all much better off, but still. Getting laid-off blows, even if you're not crazy about your job.

A few days after my layoff, when I'd gone through the roller coaster of emotions (from "I'm screwed" to "This is the best thing that ever happened to me" to "I guess I'll move back to Texas and try and get my old high school job at Hungry's Café back"), I got a call from my grandfather—a wonderful, very blunt man we called Big Papa. Grandparents are there to coddle you and tell you how special you are and let you stay up past your bedtime as a kid eating Neapolitan ice cream and watching *Benny Hill* reruns. At least, some grandparents are that way.

Big Papa: *Hi, darling. I heard the news.*

DG: *Yeah, it happened on Tuesday. But I really think it'll be for the* *best. I think it's time to do something new anyway, so maybe this is a positive thing.*

Big Papa: *Dina, darling?*

DG: *Yes?*

Big Papa: *I want to ask you something.*

DG: *OK.*

Big Papa: *Do you have any hope?*

I adored my grandfather, but "do you have any hope" is one of those questions you never, ever ask a newly laid-off person. How the hell was I supposed to answer that? I hadn't even discovered the inspirational wisdom of Snooki yet. I was still lost at sea, alone with my *Us Weekly* magazines and my terror.

I wasn't sure how to answer. I guess I had an iota or a little microscopic speck of hope because I'd gotten out of bed and brushed my teeth that day, but I wasn't quite sure what to say at that exact moment. It was too soon. "What are you going to do with all that free time" is tough to answer as well. Um, I don't know. Sleep? Cry? Watch *General Hospital*? Poke my eyeballs out with a red-hot poker? When you go from a steady job to a steady string of aimless days, time takes on a new shape. It was once structured, like the gridded squares of a calendar, and now it's amorphous, ominous, and waiting to be filled. It's terrifying, at least for those first few days.

Eventually you will have some hope. You'll find ways to fill your time (applying for jobs is a good start), and if you push hard and put effort into it, things will get better. I'm not saying it'll all be wonderful and you'll be richer and become a CEO. Maybe you'll have to take a pay cut, maybe you'll wind up babysitting or waiting tables again. But you will be working. In time. I hope it's a short amount of time. If you are going through a layoff, here are some survival tips that helped me get through the dark, dark days when I was contemplating not getting out of bed and brushing my teeth because . . . where the hell did I have to go that day?

Give yourself a break. You should start looking for work immediately after a layoff, but I think it's healthy to also allow yourself a week or so to just . . . be. I didn't have a family or kids to think about and I did get some severance, so I was fortunate in that way, but if you've been working hard for a long time and you're suddenly cut loose, don't beat yourself up for reading a magazine at noon or spending half an hour staring out the window at your crazy neighbor who walks around with her pet cockatiel on her shoulder. What the hell else do you have to do? Try and embrace those moments where you're staring into space with a blank brain. You might even miss them a tiny bit when you're back at work.

Negotiate. If you're getting laid-off—as opposed to getting fired for screaming at the boss or stealing one too many rolls of toilet paper—you need to try and negotiate some sort of severance package. Very often a company has layoffs because of financial difficulty, so unless you were in a senior position it's unlikely you'll get three- or six-months' severance. Even so, it doesn't hurt to ask for a month, two weeks—hell, a week is better than nothing. Also make sure you're paid for any unused vacation and sick days, and reread the contract you originally signed with the company to triple-check that they don't owe you any more money. My contract said that I was to be paid a certain amount for each project I brought into the company, and I made sure I got that check before I said sayonara forever.

Make a plan. A layoff is the perfect time to reassess your goals and priorities. Obviously your main concern is to make money and survive, but take the time to figure out what you truly want. Do you want to do the same type of work for the next decade, or should you switch it up? And please don't take out a bunch of loans and go hide away in graduate school to avoid reality. That is a bad plan. And don't feel that you're above certain jobs either. You need to work, so keep your ego in check.

If you have a grander plan than babysitting, then take steps to move toward making that happen every single day—while you're babysitting.

Be spontaneous. This is a good time to open yourself up to new experiences. I filled out an online application to be a contestant on *The Bachelor* when I was newly laid-off, at the urging of my sister. "You need to apply! That would be so fun seeing you on TV!" she said. I did see an upside to the idea: if I got on the show, I could finally understand her cryptic Monday night Facebook status updates like, I HATE CHELSEY SHE IS A BITCH! BUT AMY P IS SWEET I HOPE HE PICKS HER!! I did get a phone interview but that's as far as it went. After the call I realized I should have tried to act and sound more unhinged, more like a drunken stalker with daddy issues. The rejection was a good thing though because I was so confused and desperate at that point that I may have gone through with it if they'd offered me the "job." So, thank you ABC, for saving me from myself. What did I get from this spontaneous act of lunacy? I was entertained for a little while I guess, and when your days and nights need filling, entertaining yourself is a pretty important survival skill.

Be bold. Some would say that applying for *The Bachelor* is bold. I don't know who those people are, but I'm sure three or four of them exist. But since you're in the midst of this life-changing experience, why not speak your mind, take chances, apply for jobs that may have intimidated you before, or go after that career you've always been passionate about but have been too scared to try? Just make sure you're also thinking about how to make rent and pay bills. It's a balance.

Don't give in. One of the unfortunate consequences of a layoff (besides the obvious downsides) is the PTSD factor. Even if you have been bold and taken chances, when you do finally get another job that provides you with a paycheck and health insurance, there's a good chance you'll find yourself clinging to that gig for dear life, no matter how they treat you. The fear of losing the money and the benefits again is real, and it's scary, and it can turn you into a pushover. Maybe under normal circumstances, you'd be asking for a raise or a promotion, but because you're so terrified of going through a layoff again you keep your mouth shut. Or maybe they're asking you to work extra hours or weekends, but you've convinced yourself that setting boundaries will only cause them to invite you to a pancake breakfast one morning. I understand this fear all too well, and it sucks. You should always stand up for yourself though, and ask for a raise if that's in order. Just be respectful and confident, and don't let those memories of the days you were being asked, "What are you going to do with all that free time," turn you into a timid automaton. The best answer to that question, which is hard to know when you're in the midst of it all, is, "I'm going to fill it. Somehow."

44

YOU MAY BE DESPERATE FOR WORK, BUT THAT DOESN'T MEAN YOU SHOULD JOIN A CULT

Combing through Craigslist job listings during the Great Recession of 2010 was a little like looking for a monogamous relationship at a World Polyamory convention. During that wonderful time, when I'd exhausted my legit job boards for the day, I'd hop over to Craigslist to see what kinds of employment opportunities were being offered. Desperate times call for desperate measures, and that pretty much sums up the function of Craigslist. That should be their slogan. "Craigslist: Desperate Times Call for Desperate Measures." I can see the billboards in my head right now.

It wasn't all bad, actually. I got a freelance job blogging for a lamp store through Craigslist and a quick gig writing dialogue for a burlesque show.

"Have you written 1930s burlesque dialogue before?" asked the businessman-turned–theater-producer who interviewed me for the job.

"I know 1930s dialogue, and I love Bob Fosse," was my reply, which made no sense and which was a little bit of a white lie, except for the Bob Fosse part. I guess that was good enough because after the call I found myself Googling "1930s slang" and writing subtle dialogue like, "Fellas, I am gonna make it *very hard* for you to leave our little show!" I don't think the play was ever staged, but I got paid, and I got to use words like "hoosegow," "gobble pipe," and "sawbuck." In addition to the burlesque-writing gig, I also saw a few jobs for go-go dancers on Craigslist, which, on especially desperate days, was a little enticing. My favorite job description read: Visionary leader on a quest searching for a squire. I was tempted to apply just to see what kind of grifter was behind such a whimsical racket, but I figured it could only end with my photo splashed all over the evening news above the headline: Desperate, Out-of-Work Woman Slain by Visionary Leader from Craigslist. Dying at the hands of a Renaissance reenactor seemed like a bad way to go, so I never applied.

When you feel yourself getting desperate for work, it's important to know your limits so you don't end up working for con artists or quacks. Go back to babysitting, have another garage sale, work at your Uncle Melvin's sewage treatment plant—but, whatever you do, do not join a cult. I know a lot of companies seem cult*ish*, but I'm talking about actual cults, where they steal your soul, teach you to call the CEO a "visionary," and turn you into an automaton. I guess that still sounds like a lot of companies. Any company that forces employees into "team building" exercises could be considered slightly cultish, but they could still be on the up and up. It's your duty to learn to differentiate between the cult and the cultish.

> **When you feel yourself getting desperate for work, it's important to know your limits so you don't end up working for con artists or quacks.**

To explain the difference between a regular old cult-y corporation and an actual cult, I'll tell you about my own run-in with a creepy group of people that I'm 99 percent sure were in a cult. Hopefully it will demonstrate why you should proceed with caution when answering Craigslist job postings, and why you should never work for a dogmatic weirdo who wants to obliterate your soul.

This particular job called for a blogger to write about a "miracle" health pill, which seemed normal enough, especially in Los Angeles. I applied, got an interview, and drove to a warehouse on the outskirts of downtown. After a few minutes in the waiting room—which I spent trying to refresh Twitter on my iPhone even though I had no reception because god forbid I just sit and disconnect for a minute—I was greeted by a tatted-up wisp of a man with jet-black hair. He wasn't paper thin, but from the side his body was no wider than a box of vermicelli. His big dark eyes seemed sad as we shook hands. Well, I shook his hand and he just sort of suspended his clammy metacarpus in my palm. He said his name was Gabe, and then he told me to follow him up a narrow staircase. I walked behind him trying to erase the memory of the traumatic handshake I'd just experienced. At the top of the stairs we entered a large room with industrial-sized shelves that were crammed with multicolored headbands. "I didn't know you guys made accessories too," I wittily observed. I was taught that small talk is better than no talk. My grandmother would have asked a monk who'd sworn a vow of silence where his momma was born and whether he liked jalapeño poppers. Gabe looked at me with his big, dark eyes, bowed his head a little, and reverently said, "Yes. We sell headbands too." Gabe infused that sentiment with aching melancholy, turning a stylish inanimate object into a universal symbol of sorrow.

I frantically searched my brain for something to talk about besides headbands or handshakes when a black-haired, tatted-up woman entered the room and interrupted the rapturous convo I was having with Gabe. "I'm Claire, Gabe's wife. We're so glad you could make it!" Unlike Gabe, Claire stuck her hand out for a firm shake.

"It's good to meet you!" I said in my best interview voice, which I try to keep somewhere between "phony" and "deceased." We sat around a table, and Claire spoke while Gabe jotted down notes. It was hard to focus on what she was saying because I kept wondering why Gabe was taking so many notes, and whether he was faking taking notes.

"We believe in this product. L+E, which stands for Life and Energy, is a-ma-zing," Claire gushed, extending every syllable in *amazing* so I would know it was amazing in that orgasmic way that only members of a cult seem to experience. "It's really Justin's passion—you'll see when you meet him. Justin is the founder. The way he talks about L+E is so transformative. I take the vitamins every day, and it has really changed my life. What do you do to stay healthy and work out, Dina?" she asked. I'd never been asked about my exercise regimen in a job interview, so I just blurted out the truth.

"I do Billy Blanks kickboxing DVDs in my apartment."

"Well, you're perfect for the job," Claire said. Gabe scribbled some more notes and then, out of nowhere, He appeared. For all their devotion to L+E, Claire and Gabe were not really the picture of health. They looked like they'd be more comfy in a meth lab than in a gym. But when Justin sauntered in, he made them look like Gwyneth Paltrow in comparison. He wore a shiny grey suit jacket and jeans. His eyes were bloodshot and soupy, and little beads of sweat dotted his red face. In a nightclub at three in the morning he'd look pretty normal; in a sunny warehouse at ten in the morning, he looked like a guy who had secrets. Cult-y secrets.

Claire and Gabe immediately stood at attention, and I felt the energy in the room shift, as if Ming the Merciless had just waltzed into the headband factory.

"Hi Justin, can we get you anything?" This was Gabe, taking a break from his notebook to kowtow. Justin raised his hand in a gesture that I guess meant, *Not now, underling*, because Gabe didn't rush to get him anything.

"Justin, this is Dina, our new writer," Claire said. This bitch had just made a big decision for me, without my consent. But, alas, I was unemployed and in need of a job, so I just kept my mouth shut like the desperate hireling that I was. Once the introductions ended, Justin sat, so we all sat. There was an awkward silence, and Justin took a big, deep, important breath.

"I had a Galileo Moment," Justin began. I had no idea what he was talking about but I was all ears. "From that Galileo Moment, we created this." His arm swept across the empty table. He could as easily have been talking about the headbands on the shelves as about life itself. "Have you ever had a Galileo Moment, Dina?" he asked.

"I'm not sure," I answered.

"Interesting," he said, taking another big, deep, important breath.

"I need you—the Writer—to translate our Message from the mountaintop to the masses. What we are doing is revolutionary. L+E will transform people's lives. You can take L+E after you've been drinking until four in the morning, partying . . ." This elicits chuckles from Justin, Gabe, and Claire, which made me uncomfortable but I fake-laughed along anyway. "You will feel incredible. It's like the metaphor of lighting the candle with no fire."

I tried to imagine what this metaphor might mean. Was it about magic? Was Justin saying he had superpowers? Maybe they were arsonists. All I knew was that he looked more like a guy who had been on a bender than a guy whose superhuman powers enabled him to light candles with his mind.

"This is a Movement," Justin went on. "It is going to change people's lives, and I need you to tell them that, and tell my story without, well, I don't want to . . ."

"You don't want to scare people away, so you want to ease them in?" I asked. Maybe I shouldn't have interrupted Justin, but I felt tense, and blurting things out has been proven to release tension—and then, usually, recreate that tension, times ten.

There was a long pause. I tried to come up with ways to defend myself if they decided to lock me in a trunk full of headbands for insulting Justin and his miracle pills.

"*Yes*," he finally said. "Yes, and not scare them away. We need to tell the people what we've discovered here but without scaring them away. People fear Truth," Justin said. Claire and Gabe chanted "mmmhmmm" and "that's right." At that moment I figured the safest thing to do would be to pretend to take the job and then bolt.

The pay was actually pretty good, and a little tempting, but there was no way I was going to fill out tax forms and hand them over to these people.

"Let's start Monday," Justin said. "Which location shall we meet at?"

"The Summit?" Claire offered. I had no idea what The Summit was but it sounded like a place where they locked you in windowless concrete rooms and taught you about the Galileo Moment.

"Perfect. We'll start Monday, 9:00 AM, at The Summit," Justin agreed. Gabe the human vermicelli box scribbled notes. For all I knew, he could have been writing an SOS.

"That sounds great," I said. Then Justin reached into his coat pocket, pulled out a square tin, and pressed it into my palm. It said "L+E" on the top, and pills jangled inside. "Take these," Justin said. "Take three a day—you need to know the product. It will change your life. You're going to be transformed."

"I'm so excited!" I said, lying as if my life depended on it. That's not a dramatic flourish. These people were lunatics.

After a few quick goodbyes I hurried to my car and drove home. I hadn't accepted the job, but I did say I was excited and that I'd think about it in a very enthused way. To be honest, a little part of me was tempted to write blog posts for Justin, Claire, and Gabe. If you're laid-off and unemployed, it's tough to be rational. I went over the pros and cons of the job as I drove back across town.

Pros: *Money*

Cons: *Losing your identity and soul, shutting your family and everyone you love out of your life, learning about The Galileo Moment, Gabe's handshakes, The Summit, being murdered by Justin*

When I got home I immediately called the best and worst person I could think to tell this story to: my conspiracy-theory-loving friend, Mark. Mark believes that news anchors are aliens if you can find a YouTube video of them that pixilates.

"Do not take those," Mark whispered, as if the phones were

tapped. "There's an urban myth about this South American drug scopolamine. That might be what they gave you—it's a mind eraser. Call the cops, or throw it out. But *stay away*."

His hysteria stoked my own penchant for melodrama, so I started Googling scopolamine, convinced they'd given me a mind-erasing drug so I would zombie-walk to the Summit on Monday morning wearing a bonnet and chanting Justin's name. Everything I read about scopolamine sounded serious. Supposedly criminals dosed hapless victims with the stuff, and it would temporarily erase their brains. The criminals could then do things like take them to an ATM, say, "Put in your pin, withdraw $500, and hand it over," and they'd do it and never remember that it happened.

Scopolamine was also described as having a putrid scent, so I opened the L+E tin to smell the pills. They smelled like black licorice and dirt, and that was putrid enough for me. Despite Mark's advice, I wasn't going to call the LAPD—that didn't sound promising. For a brief second I wondered if I should stop being a baby and try the pills, since this could be my Hunter S. Thompson moment. I'm not Hunter S. Thompson though. He was adventurous and probably didn't have a mom who said, "Don't go in the water you'll get eaten by a shark!" every time he said he was going to the beach or to a small landlocked puddle.

I emailed Gabe and Claire, politely thanked them for their time, and told them the job wasn't for me. The phone rang four minutes later. It was Gabe. He was worried that they'd done something to offend me and begged me to reconsider and go to The Summit. "We really felt a connection with you," he said. I firmly said no thanks, and when he'd exhausted all his brainwashing techniques he said, "Well, we need the pills back. Can you bring them tomorrow?" Hell no I could not bring them tomorrow. I could maybe mail them though. We hung up, and I got a few pleading follow-up emails from Claire, which I ignored.

I called Mark for advice. If I mailed the pills, Justin could give them to the next Writer, and I'd be free. "Don't put them in the mail unless you want to wind up on a terrorist watch list," Mark said. "Throw them in the trash."

"But what if a squirrel or a bird eats them?" I asked. "What if animals start going crazy and there's some weird outbreak?" The thought of being responsible for an infestation of cult-like squirrels or crows in Los Angeles County was upsetting.

I said goodbye to Mark and stared at the L+E tin, as if at any moment a genie would pop out and tell me what to do. Eventually I realized that Justin, Claire, and Gabe might be in a cult, but they didn't have any power over me, and I could do whatever I wanted. I mustered up some courage, picked up the little tin of miracle pills, and chucked them into the dumpster behind my apartment. There were no animals in sight, but I whispered, "I'm sorry," just in case.

Maybe L+E pills are little miracles, not mind-erasing drugs. Maybe I would have made a ton of money convincing people that Justin is a messiah. I was desperate for work, but not desperate enough to get mixed up in that mess. It turns out, throwing that tin away and turning that job down was my Galileo Moment. Making money and working is important, but it's also important to know your boundaries and steer clear of the Justins of the world, and anyone who claims to be a Visionary Leader on a quest in search of a squire. Bosses can be crazy, but you need to differentiate between everyday, normal crazy and out-of-their-mind, soul-sucking cult-leader crazy. Sometimes it's not so easy to tell the difference.

45

POP QUIZ: HOW TO TELL A REAL PARTY FROM A PYRAMID-SCHEME PARTY

pyr·a·mid scheme [PEER-*rah*-mid SKEEM]: a dishonest and usually illegal business in which many people are persuaded to invest their money and the money of later investors is used to pay the people who invested first[20]

pyr·a·mid [PEER-*rah*-mid]: a very large structure build especially in ancient Egypt that has a square base and four triangular sides which form a point at the top. 2. a shape, object, or pile that is wide near the bottom and narrows gradually as it reaches the top[21]

---

20. By permission. From Merriam-Webster's Collegiate® Dictionary, 11th Edition ©2014 by Merriam-Webster, Inc. (www.Merriam-Webster.com).
21. Ibid.

This is a test.

1. An acquaintance, friend, or stranger says, "I made $5,000 last month selling socks that reverse the aging process while you sleep. You want to get in on this? The owner is having a party so you should come." This party is

   ☐ Legit
   ☐ A pyramid-scheme party

2. You go to a girls/guys night out and you notice a conspicuous display of vitamins/miracle creams/dayglo energy drinks in the center of the table along with guidebooks explaining how you can make $5,000 a month and get a year's supply of power suits just by selling the vitamins/miracle creams/dayglo energy drinks. This party is

   ☐ Legit
   ☐ A pyramid-scheme party

3. You're on the dance floor, shaking your ass to Macklemore because you've had so many margaritas you mistakenly think the DJ is playing *the best song ever* when the music screeches to a halt and a very attractive man or woman grabs a microphone and says, "Are you guys having a good time?! I hope so because what I'm about to tell you will CHANGE YOUR LIFE!" This party is

   ☐ Legit
   ☐ A pyramid-scheme party

4. It's Saturday night and you walk into a party and spot stacks of pamphlets strategically scattered around the room. Everyone is extremely happy. You notice the cover of the pamphlet shows a man on a sailboat smoking a cigar and says, "Work from home and double your money." This party is

   ☐ Legit
   ☐ A pyramid-scheme party

Now, take a moment to tally up your answers. If you checked "Legit" for any of the questions, you need to guard your wallet with your life and stay alert because you're a prime target for a pyramid scheme, Ponzi scheme, or their more innocuous-sounding cousin, the multilevel marketing opportunity. If someone asks you to pay a fee in order to work for them, you should put on your trilby hat, grab your magnifying glass, and dig into their history. If you've ever been asked to "go in on" an investment or a business deal, don't be surprised if you eventually find yourself broke, behind bars, and telling a poker-faced judge, "But I was just trying to make a living, Your Honor!" And if you catch yourself running to Western Union every time you get an email with the subject line HELLO MY DEAREST ONE from a person in Abidjan, Cote d'Ivoire, named Miss Christine Smith who needs money to transfer USD $3,500,000.00 from a bank account left by her dear departed father who was killed during the "President Gbagbo time," you need to get a hold of yourself, and your money.

If you're looking to get rich quick, the first step is to erase the word "quick" from that phrase. Most of the billionaires and millionaires of this world worked hard to get to the point where they could build a yacht that has white stingray-hide wallpaper, commission a bespoke Swarovski claw-foot bathtub for $40,000, or buy the world's most expensive pool cue: the $150,000 Intimidator from McDermott Handcrafted Cues. If your goal is to become filthy rich, but your path to caviar facials and Lamborghini Aventadors involves shortcuts, scams, schemes, or shell games of any kind, there's a good chance you'll be giving that Lamborghini to the government when the jig is up. No one likes toiling away day after day, but the old saying is true: if it sounds too good to be true, it probably is.

Take the movie *Working Girl*. Melanie Griffith plays Tess, a big-haired, shoulder-pad-clad secretary from the wrong side of the tracks (a.k.a. Staten Island) who makes her way to a corner office in Manhattan through grit, ingenuity, and hard work, not by scheming and scamming and lending money to Miss Christine Smith from Abidjan, Cote d'Ivoire. She didn't get to "run shit"—like my friend Bane the intern dreamed of doing—by skipping steps. She made a plan, took action, trusted her gut, and asserted herself by saying snappy things like, "I am not a steak—you can't just order me!" Tess might not have gotten so rich that she could buy a small island or build a rocket so she could shoot into space and start a hotel chain there, but she achieved a dream and bettered her situation through hard work, not through whining about hard work. Pyramid schemes and get-rich-quick scams are pretty wimpy ways to make a buck. Getting ahead through hard work is sexy, and if you take that route, you're much less likely to find the fuzz knocking on the door of your house or yacht or personalized spaceship with a warrant and some handcuffs.

It's not as simple as that, though. Hard work does not always equal success, especially in today's world. Sometimes—oftentimes—hard work equals days and months and years of busting your ass trying to get ahead and finding that you're still waking up in the same spot. But a futon in a tiny apartment is a hell of a lot cozier than a cot in the pokey. Neither one is probably as cozy as a $50,000 Monarch Vi-Spring bed that has over 3,000 springs, but *c'est la vie*. No one ever died from not sleeping in a $50,000 handcrafted bed. They may have pouted a little, but they definitely didn't die.

VIII.

LOVE AND RELATIONSHIPS

My bounty is as boundless as the sea. My love as deep. The more I give to thee, the more I have, for both are infinite.
—Shakespeare, Romeo and Juliet

Love is wonderful, but when money goes out the window, love usually flies out right along with it.
—Eddie Fay Horton (a.k.a. my grandmother)

46

NOBODY WRITES ODES ABOUT ROMANCE AND FINANCE

I am sitting at a sidewalk café with my love—he is dark with dark blue eyes. We are sitting in black iron chairs drinking tea. The weather is chilly but sunny; the sky is vibrant blue. There are flower and fruit stands along the street, children run about laughing. It is midmorning. My lover and I are fresh and relaxed—we spent the night making silent, stormy love. We are quiet, but we talk of oceans. We are barefoot. I am a writer; he is a painter. We ride horses, eat berries of the sweetest vine, breathe air sent from the heavens. We shower outside, ride bicycles everywhere, we meet old couples who tell us endless stories. The man living next to us plays his guitar each night on his balcony—the music weaves through the air to our room . . . someday.

This Pulitzer-worthy passage wasn't written by Pablo Neruda or Anaïs Nin. Unfortunately, it was written by me, in tenth grade, when I was a virginal *Flowers in the Attic* fan who thought that dark blue eyes were the ultimate and that normal, everyday people actually made silent, stormy love. I even sketched a picture of this idyllic locale with black iron chairs, which is now fading away in an old journal. Only virgins call sex "making love," and only naive kids who have never balanced a checkbook think that an artist and a writer running around barefoot and eating berries is a sane vision of romantic bliss. Breathing "air sent from the heavens" is ridiculous, but when you grow up believing that when it comes to romance, drinking poison and stabbing yourself in the heart with a dagger is preferable to living without love, it's an excusable offense. Sort of. Thank you, William Shakespeare.

With a little life under my belt and a few relationships in my rearview, my teen vision of romantic bliss sounds like a pretty nice vacation, but if that were my everyday relationship, I'd probably wind up in a straitjacket. You'd get bored listening to the old couple's endless stories. Not only that, those iron chairs would probably tweak your sciatic nerve and leave you with a waffle-patterned ass after a few heavenly encounters. When you're in the la-la land of your teens and early twenties, making stormy love and waxing poetic about art and nature and the vastness of the cosmos seems like it's enough to sustain a relationship. Step into the real world, though, and you realize that any rapturous, all-night conversations about Frida Kahlo or Kurt Cobain eventually lead to groggy, early morning conversations about when the rent is due.

That's perfectly fine, as long as you and your barefoot lover with the dark blue eyes can handle both types of talks with maturity and love. Plus, don't you usually get the philosophical "deep" conversations out of your system by about your early- or midtwenties? There's only so much wonderment a person can take before you start craving a romantic night on the couch eating pizza and watching *Seinfeld* reruns. If a grown man poured me a glass of Sancerre and asked, "What's your feeling about Yeats's poetry?" I would think that he was either an associate literature professor who wasn't very well-rounded, or that he was suffering from some sort of stunted growth syndrome. A man-child stuck in the glory days of twentieth-century Irish lit class.

At some point in life, usually when you're in your late twenties or early thirties, that type of talk ceases to sound romantic and starts to sound like a warning bell: "This person will one day quote Proust while you're arguing about the gas bill." Heed its call. Talking about money is frustrating and it's real—you cannot make it poetic or romantic unless your name is Bob Dylan, which it probably is not. The rest of us have to discuss finances and rocky relationship moments without the help of a harmonica.

Poetic love ballads and romantic comedies are wonderful because they give us an escape and take us to a land where love conquers all and either everyone has a convenient, mysterious amount of wealth, emotions trump economics, or money just doesn't exist. If the romantic movie is a musical, they'll also throw in operatic odes to all-consuming love that lead you to believe that if two people can dance and sing on rooftops like Christian and Satine in *Moulin Rouge!*, everything will be just fine. It's a nice fairy tale, but in real life, Christian and Satine would also need to talk about practical things like rent or mortgages. And at least one of them would need to have a decent credit score. You cannot buy a house by wowing a realtor with your dazzling dance moves.

You may be madly in love, but if you're a spender who dreams of mansions and your soul mate is a saver content in a two-bedroom townhouse, you need to take those differences seriously.

At some point you and your beloved will have to talk about paying the plumber or discuss how much it'll cost to regrout the tiles in the shower. The trick is to sustain the desire to make silent, stormy love after all the libido-crushing financial foreplay and to make sure you both have the same approach to finances. You may be madly in love, but if you're a spender who dreams of mansions and your soul mate is a saver content in a two-bedroom townhouse, you need to take those differences seriously. I'm not saying it won't work out, but you'll need to discuss it and find ways to compromise and make it work.

My Southern belle grandmother, Eddie Fay—a.k.a. Mamaw—grew up on a farm and brought goats home on the school bus. (Think country Southern belle rather than Scarlett O'Hara or NeNe Leakes.) When it came to love and marriage, Mamaw's motto was:

"Love is wonderful, but when money goes out the window, love usually flies out right along with it." She adored and loved my grandfather, a talented artist who worked double shifts on the railroad all his life, but she was also a practical woman, and she understood that the last thing you want when you're trying to raise a family or you're struggling financially is for your spouse to quit their job and give slam poetry a whirl. She didn't have any illusions about what it takes to sustain a relationship. Nor did my grandfather want to quit the railroad to become the next Degas. They were on the same page and there was no resentment.

Thinking about money does kind of kill the romance, which is probably why our early relationships are usually so dramatic and soaring and explosive. Financial guru Alvin Hall has said that money is more important than sex when it comes to relationships." I guess that depends on the sex, but there's truth in what he's saying. Back in high school, I thought that gazing meaningfully into your lover's eyes was the cosmic bond that held two people together, but now I realize Hall is right. The ability to weather awkward, sometimes painful discussions about finances in a relationship is just as important as two bodies and souls comingling as one—it's just way less romantic, obviously.

It is important to value love over money, but you should also realize that love alone cannot sustain a relationship. My grandmother's "love flies out the window" motto might sound less romantic than a Neruda poem, so maybe to make it a little more dreamy we can alter it to go like this: "Love is wonderful, but when money goes out the window, love sometimes flies out right along with it if you don't know how to calmly, compassionately discuss finances with your soul mate."

Talking about money with someone you love can be painful, but if you proceed with kindness, take deep breaths, and remember that as long as you are both trying, you cannot make the other person feel guilty about money, you should be able to balance the romance and the finance. And if you're able to live out that fantasy of making silent, stormy love and eating berries of the sweetest vine, have at it. Just don't forget to pay the rent on your quaint villa and tip the waiter who brings out your ambrosial cups of tea. Skimping in either scenario could take the celestial wind out of your and your honey's sails pretty quickly, and instead of being blissful lovers basking in the sunlight, you'll turn into the woebegone couple bickering about the one thing no one writes euphoric love poems about—money.

47

THE LOVE LIST

very guru from the Dalai Lama to Dolly Parton believes in the power of intention. You put something out there to the universe, some positive thought or desire, and—poof!—there it is. Just close your eyes, concentrate, and envision yourself holding an Oscar, finding true love, or landing on one of those "30 Under 30" lists in your chosen field, and by sheer force of will, you're one step closer to your dream. There are no charts and graphs proving that the power of intention works, but if it's good enough for Dolly Parton, it's good enough for me. Tossing a hopeful, positive thought out there is better than stewing in a vat of self-sabotage and cynicism, but just don't get *too* positive. If you're running around like a Pollyanna quoting *The Secret* everywhere you go, a healthy dose of cynicism is probably in order. Brokenomics is about balance, and sometimes that means evening the scales between blind optimism and subtle rancor until you find your happy/cautiously optimistic place.

Unlike our ancient ancestors, we have options when looking for love. You can sign up for Tinder or enroll in some speed-dating sessions. You can leave it to fate and wait until the day you "meet cute" with your future husband or wife in a bookstore or at the farmers' market while you're examining organic kumquats. If you approach every day as if it's a rom-com, you'll both grab *the same exact kumquat* and instantly fall in love, but you'll bicker and pretend you can't stand each other for a while because that adds tension and it's more dramatic. Then in the third act you're sad and dejected, so you go to the kumquat stand all alone one drizzly Sunday. By some miracle, the clouds part, a rainbow appears, you see your enemy/soul mate, profess your love just as an elderly couple strolls by hand in hand, kiss (a sudden breeze knocks the fedora off your head but you don't care!), recite a quotable monologue that sounds like it was written by a disgruntled screenwriter, and then get married six months later under a kumquat tree.

If that sounds too complicated, there's always the get-drunk-at-a-bar-and-take-home-a-random-stranger-hoping-your-one-night-stand-turns-into-a-lasting-love option, which is not the most feasible or romantic tactic, although it has been known to work on rare occasions. Or, if you're really reaching, you can comb through every horoscope from *Elle* magazine to Astrology-Zone.com until you find one that prophesizes you will find love in June because Mercury and Venus are tilting or spinning in a certain way. The next step is to spend the month passively waiting around for a Scorpio-Cancer miracle. Like joining a cult, religiously reading your horoscope seems to happen during phases when you're feeling the most vulnerable and needy, but you won't find that fascinating fact in any astrological profile. If you come across enough sentences saying, "This month keep your eyes open for that special someone," and you're continually meeting commitment-phobic narcissists, you eventually, hopefully, stop obsessively researching your astrological love matches and take action, get proactive, and write a list. A love list. A list of things you want in a lifetime lover.

My friends and I started making these lists as soon as our Holy Grail of Womanhood (*Seventeen* magazine) told us it was a great way to conjure up a soul mate. This was our low-tech version of the experiment conducted by the two nerdy guys in *Weird Science*. If you're unfamiliar with this classic film, Wyatt (Ilan

Mitchell-Smith, who seems to have gotten out of the acting racket) and Gary (Anthony Michael Hall) magically, with the help of the latest 1980s technology, create their dream girl: a hot British chick who appears in a smoky neon pink doorway wearing a crop top and underwear. They do this by typing the traits they want in a soul mate (boobs, legs, pretty face, the end) into their giant computer. Then, channeling Einstein, they put bras on their heads and wait. Unlike Wyatt and Gary, my friends and I kept it simple and used a piece of paper and multicolored pens to cast our spells. Girls are more mature than boys, and we would not have been caught dead with bras on our heads. We were mortified by those things even when they were hidden underneath our T-shirts. Also, we didn't have a computer.

And so, brimming with hope and hormones, my friends and I formed a club of three called the "PTKs," (Pre-Teen Knockouts). The club was exclusive, and our spiritual totem was a pink spiral notebook, in which we wrote our lists and glued photos of ourselves, writing PTKs underneath each picture in flowery pink-and-blue captions. For awkward preteens with braces and headgear, we still managed to act like a bunch of arrogant assholes. I like to think we just didn't know any better, since middle school is teeming with assholes. The key is to claw your way out of there and evolve into a decent person who does not sit around sticking pictures of herself into a notebook like a demented pageant queen.

Thanks to the magazines we all read, we knew we should crimp our hair to really make a lasting impression. We learned that if we stuck a pencil under one of our boobs and it fell to the floor (the pencil, not our boob), we had a perfect, perky rack like the model; but if the pencil stayed lodged in the fleshy environs between our boob and our ribcage, we had horrible old-lady breasts, and no one would ever love us or want to see us naked. In addition to making us feel like twelve-year-old ogres who were past our prime even though we were barely out of training bras, the magazines also helped us realize that we needed to get serious about our love lists if we were actually going to meet the *perfect man*. You can call it your "Things I Want In a Man/Woman" list, if you want to be more specific. All through junior high school, my perfect-man list went like this:

Things I Want In a Man:

- Handsome
- Good Body
- Artistic
- Good Kisser
- Sweet
- Good Dresser
- Tall
- Six-Pack

That's it. Those are important qualities, for the most part, even though the older you get things like "good body" and "good dresser" take a backseat to new and improved additions like "honest" and "employed." Show me a kind, selfless, goofy, employed person with a six-pack (famous actors don't count—they're not real people, they're basically holograms) and I'll show you a gorgeous size-two woman in a sports jersey who wolfs down double cheeseburgers while simultaneously telling the world's most hilarious dirty joke, giving a lecture on astrophysics, cooking lasagna, and adding expert picks to her Fantasy Football league.

Maybe you like handlebar mustaches or dream of meeting someone who shares your passion for gnawing giant turkey legs at the Renaissance Pleasure Faire. Some people want a woman who wears stilettos and hot pants, and others dream of meeting a dreadlocked girl named Raven who wears body paint and Birkenstocks at the local drum circle. What you put on your list is your choice, but if a 6'2" billionaire with six-pack abs and a Bahamian bank account are the only items on your list, we need to do some retooling. For example, "Is willing to replace a lightbulb" is much better than "Won't change a lightbulb but loves maxing out a black Amex." Of course, someone with a black Amex would probably pay someone to replace a lightbulb, but you get the idea.

When crafting your list you need to be as specific as possible. As you plow through relationships and learn from your mistakes, your list will hopefully evolve and change. For example, if you date a vegan accountant with platinum blonde hair who turns out to be a nightmare, your next list might have things like, "Jet black hair," "Unabashed carnivore," and "Professional ballet dancer." A tall, reserved meditation enthusiast who winds up becoming a serial texter could prompt you to put "Medium height," "Hyper," and "Irreverent" on your next list. A lot of these are superficial traits, obviously, and they don't mean as much as the inner qualities of a soul mate. They're still fun to add, though, and listing traits that are the polar opposite of your last lover is a great way to release a little pent-up anger about an ex. It may be immature, but you're doing this in secret, behind closed doors—or if you're not, you should be—so it's fine to be a little childish. And who isn't a little childish after a breakup? I bet Winston Churchill and General George S. Patton even got a little cray-cray after bad breakups. There's no existing historical documentation about their love lists, though, which is too bad.

When it comes to the inner traits you want in a mate, some wise additions to your "Toned abs" list could include:

- Kind

- Responsible

- Generous

- Communicates well

- Honest

- Open-minded

- Thoughtful

- Employed, or trying really hard to be employed

- Confident

- Independent

- Good Listener

- Faithful (unless you're a polyamorous type)

- Will be there when things are tough

- Is smart with money

- Has integrity

- Does not overspend on La Mer, couture clothes, or caviar

- Loves animals

- Knows how to discuss finances without having a meltdown

- Does not quote Proust when you bring up the bills

- Patient

- Puts up with you

One quick caveat: please don't write these love lists thinking that they're a foolproof way to meet the love of your life. You can have hope that they're helping, but really, they're more about you, and about being honest with yourself about what you want in a husband/wife/partner/lover. Maybe all you care about is meeting a hot, rich, toned, tall person who owns yachts and small islands, like Johnny Depp circa 2004, before he started going overboard with all that fringe. Just remember that you have to live with this person day in and day out, forever, or at least until you break up and find yourself writing a new list. We all get old, shrink, and lose the ability to even strive for six-pack abs, even if we do five-hundred sit-ups a day. Focus on lasting traits, like kindness, rather than fleeting ones, like "youthful, wrinkle-free skin," "the athletic ability of an Olympian," and "an epic trust fund."

If you're stuck, try and remember this when you're hiding in your bedroom secretly penning your next love list: epic trust funds can run out, mansions can get repossessed, and excessive spending can ruin even the most rapturous love affair that started so innocently way back when at the kumquat stand, because love does not happen in three adorable, neatly plotted acts. It happens in a chaotic typhoon of unpredictable, erratic vignettes that sometimes leave you spinning, which is why sitting still and writing lists sometimes helps.

48

DO NOT DATE ANYONE WHO VALUES THEIR BONG MORE THAN THEY VALUE YOU

College can be a wonderful time. Some say the college years are the best years of your life, which is ridiculous. The years between birth and kindergarten are the best years. You have no responsibilities besides learning to walk, read, use a potty, and talk; someone clothes, feeds, bathes, and babies you. You have recess and Push-Up pops. Your most stressful relationship is probably with a sibling, a pet turtle, or an imaginary friend, and money is something you're handed just because a tooth falls out.

In college you have to deal with tests, grades, hangovers, jobs, and getting to class on time. Your relationships are with people who paint their faces at football games, have no intention of settling down, and value their beer bongs and their subscriptions to *Maxim* magazine more than they value you. A typical date at my college consisted of meeting at a party, playing dominoes while drinking Keystone Light, and passing out in some bushes together. If those are the best years of our lives, I'd like a refund.

By the time I reached that supposedly halcyon era, my vision of perfect love had evolved from the high school dream of a quaint European café with a heavenly breeze to a thatched hut on a Hawaiian beach that smelled like pineapples and pikake blossoms. In both scenarios, my lover and I were running around barefoot, but since my college boyfriend, Zack, was an artist and a die-hard surfer, I assumed we would get married and move to Hawaii, not to England. We'd live in a hut (at least I grasped the fact that an artist and a writer would likely end up living in a hut or even a yurt instead of an actual house) and have a few naked surfer babies, and life would be one big fucking beach day. That fantasy imploded when I realized that Zack cared about his homemade beer bong more than he cared about me. He loved me, but he really loved that freaking beer bong.

If you're not familiar with beer bongs, here's a description to help orient you:

> Wikipedia: A beer bong is a device composed of a funnel attached to a tube used to facilitate the rapid consumption of beer. The use of a beer bong is also known as funneling.[22]

Zack quickly became known as "the beer bong guy" on campus, so I guess that made me some kind of queen by association. He'd waltz into parties with his beloved contraption draped around his neck like a pet. On a few occasions people actually cheered when he entered a room. Dating someone who accessorized with a funnel and a plastic tube would terrify me now, but at the beginning it was kind of fun. In an effort to live up to my growing celebrity status, I did some beer bong shots, or whatever the technical term is for kneeling down and ingesting an entire beer so fast that your eyes water and your cranium feels like it's swelling.

Zack and I were a team for a while, but eventually I grew tired of the beer bong. Unfortunately, Zack did not. I started to

---

22. Wikipedia contributors, "Beer bong," Wikipedia, The Free Encyclopedia, http://en.wikipedia.org/w/index.php?title=Beer_bong&oldid=614585316 (accessed December 16, 2014). Anyone who called it "funneling" would probably not be invited back to the beer bong party.

wonder how he would help take care of our surfer babies if he was beerbonging all day long. Would I be the only one cleaning our beach hut, since he'd be too busy fawning over plastic funnels? And did I want to marry a guy who wore a beer-drinking device around town? These thoughts plagued me for several months until I finally came to terms with the fact that a funnel and a tube had made me the third wheel in my relationship and it was time to cut Zack and his beer bong loose and grant them the freedom to love each other unconditionally.

We didn't break up just because of Zack's plastic pet, but it was a major contributor to our demise. It symbolized something. I'm sure Freud would have had a field day with whatever that symbol was, and he would have been wrong, because I think it just symbolized beer. Zack wasn't a bad guy, but we were immature and I guess I just became a smidgen less immature than he was, so it was time to move on. The relationship did teach me not to stay with someone who valued his beer bong more than he valued me. This is a universal truth, and the sooner you learn it the better off you will be. Here are some other things that the person you're in a relationship with should not value more than they value you:

- Their car

- Their shoes

- Their hairdo

- A cronut

- Their Rajon Rondo Celtics jersey

- A bracelet

- Peeps

- A bicycle (if you've ever dated a triathlete or a bike messenger, you know this is very possible)

- Designer handbags

- Their Blendtec Smoother Q-Series 20 amp blender

- Steroids

- Sleeping pills

- Truffles

- Their bespoke submarine

- Money

Money is great, and it would be hard not to love a designer handbag or a really cool bicycle, but if you're in a relationship and you notice that the person seems to be putting material possessions like a beer bong or a bespoke submarine before you, it's time to sit them down for a calm, rational talk about priorities. If they're not listening and they start making a smoothie with their Blendtec blender while you're talking, you should probably hit the road. If you love someone set them free, and if it turns out that they love a thing more than they love you, get out of there so you can find a healthy, wonderful relationship with a human being and they can live happily ever after with their stuff.

49

TO SUGAR DADDY/MAMA OR NOT
TO SUGAR DADDY/MAMA

My freshman roommate in college, a pretty, tall brunette named Melanie, was one of those rare birds that was actually born and raised in Los Angeles. We were the same age but Melanie was much more sophisticated than I was, mainly because Zack "the beer bong guy" and I were stumbling home on the weekends after epic sake-bomb contests, and she was gliding home in stilettos after a date at a restaurant that had cloth napkins and wine glasses that weren't made of plastic.

Even though we were living in close quarters, she kept her fancy dating life to herself for the first few months of school. Then one night as I was walking back to the dorm with my dinner in hand (a poppy seed muffin and a Coke—*bon appetit!*), I saw Melanie sitting in a shiny BMW convertible driven by a man with a full head of grey hair. This was not George Clooney or Anderson Cooper grey. This was Random Old Guy grey. I tried not to stare, but she leaned in and kissed this silver-headed man on the lips. Now, looking back, I realize he was probably barely sixty, but when you're eighteen-years-old, sixty may as well be deceased.

"Hey!" I chirped when our paths crossed on the way to our room. "I got a poppy seed muffin. Want some?" Offering her a pastry seemed like a better option than blurting, "Why were you just kissing your great-grandfather?"

Melanie looked back at Old Man River speeding away. She seemed a little embarrassed when she said, "That was Steven. My boyfriend. Sort of my boyfriend."

"He seems nice," I said, as if the ability to peel out of a college dorm roundabout in a BMW was a universal indicator of kindness.

"He's a little older than we are, but he's really good to me. He offered to pay for school. I don't know if I'll let him, but I'm thinking about it because it's a lot of money." A rogue poppy seed lodged in my throat, and I coughed, which I think Melanie took as a sign of shock and disapproval because she started talking faster. "He takes me to really nice places, and he's giving me his car next week because he's getting a new Audi. That's pretty sweet, right? I could use a car."

I agreed that it was very sweet. Hell, who wouldn't want a free BMW, as long as there were no strings attached to a man who was roughly the same age as Stonehenge?

The website SugarDaddy.com hadn't been invented yet but I had seen *Pretty Woman* fifteen times, so I wasn't totally naive about the fact that relationships like this existed. I know hooker Julia Roberts and wealthy, upper-crust Richard Gere genuinely loved each other, but if he had been a toothless beggar, would she have giggled so maniacally at that box snapping shut? I think not. I'm pretty sure she would think he was a raving, penniless lunatic who was trying to cut off her fingers so he could sell them on the black market, and she'd run away as fast as her thigh-high Frederick's of Hollywood boots would let her.

That night Melanie revealed that Steven also bought her a new wardrobe (he owned some sort of clothing company, probably made in China and financed in Abu Dhabi), took her to sushi dinners at places that didn't allow sake bombs, and really, truly cared about her. As I listened, I wondered if I, too, could date a wealthy man whose bathroom cabinets were no doubt stocked with Viagra and Cialis—a man who could afford to disguise his grey pubic hair with expensive, surreptitious salon treatments. A man who had long ago traded in his plastic beer bong for a bottle of Macallan 1926 and some crystal goblets. Melanie must have been on to me because she said, "Dina, don't judge me."

"I'm not judging you," I lied.

"Look," she said. "I was raised by my mom and we had nothing. So don't judge me for wanting some nice things, OK? You don't know what it's like."

As much as seeing Melanie in a lip-lock with John Kerry's doppelganger gave me the heebie-jeebies, I had to admit she was making sense. Who was I to judge? My boyfriend could barely afford the all-you-can-eat breadsticks and salad special at Olive Garden, which was delicious, but come on.

"You're right. Sorry. So what's he like? His personality, I mean," I asked, trying not to be so judgy and also trying to avoid a description of any part of Steven from the neck down.

"He's nice. He has a nice house too," was Melanie's full and final assessment of the man. Not, "He's funny!" or "He's really talented, and he's amazing in bed!" or "He's the most wonderful, smart, generous man I've ever met, and I can't wait to have his babies!" Instead, she told me about all the fancy things he'd promised her.

"Nice is good," I agreed. Zack was nice, despite the beer bong fixation. I still felt a little skeptical, but then a strange thing happened. The more she went into detail about her hoity-toity dinners and her trips to Santa Barbara, the sexier Steven became in my mind. It was all very alluring, especially when you're used to dining on muffins and your vacations consist of sharing a room at a Travelodge off the strip in Vegas with six friends. Melanie's secret life became my daytime soap opera. I loved hearing her stories about where she'd been, what he bought her, and the promises he was making about paying her tuition and setting her up with an apartment in West Hollywood because she deserved better than to share a dorm room with a girl who wore overalls and dated "the beer bong guy." When I saw all her new outfits I lamented the fact that we didn't wear the same size shoes or clothes. Late-night calzones and Keystone Light had rounded me out a little, from my head all the way down to my toes. The overalls made me feel sexy.

Melanie and Steven continued seeing each other for a few months, and the soap opera updates kept getting more enticing. Then one day she bounded into the dorm room as Zack and I were having a heated debate about the correct spelling of Kurt Cobain's name.

"Hi! You guys want to do something? I feel like going out!" she said.

"Are you OK?" I asked. Melanie never wanted to go out with us. She was much too fancy.

"I broke up with Steven last night. I feel like celebrating."

"Really? It seemed like it was going so well." What about my soap opera updates? I needed those. They were distracting me from my own ridiculous relationship problems and my Art History of India exam.

"Yeah, I guess it was. But he's just sort of . . . older."

I scanned Melanie's eyeballs to see if maybe she had suddenly gotten a prescription for contact lenses, since extremely blurry vision would explain her obliviousness to the fact that Steven, unlike most guys our age, had to deal with prostate checks and nose hair.

"I felt smothered. He wanted to buy me an apartment and I felt weird letting him pay for school, like I'd owe him or something, you know? I think I just want to try dating a guy my own age, even if he doesn't have money. I don't know. Maybe it won't last. I just need some space."

"Let's go out—you're single, you need to meet some dudes," Zack opined.

"Where should we go?" Melanie asked tentatively.

"Cowboy Sushi: $2 California rolls and $4 sake bombs." It was Zack's favorite spot.

"Oh. Thanks, I'm OK," Melanie said. "Maybe I'll just study." Zack was bummed, but I understood. It was too soon to jump from five-star restaurants to sake bombs and bottom-of-the-barrel sushi. She needed to ease her way back into the cheap seats.

I lost touch with Melanie after college, so who knows if she's living in Kansas City with a mild mannered paleontologist named Bert or jetting around the world with an eighty-year-old named Franklin Montpelier III, Esquire. Either way I hope she's happy.

Years later, I thought of Melanie when I had my own brush with a potential Steven, and let me tell you it was a true test of will power. This was when I'd been laid-off from my job with Stan the MFA-phobe for two months, which, as you can guess, meant that fancy vacations were about as feasible as buying a Bugatti Veyron 16.4 Grand Sport Vitesse (price: approximately $2.5 million). A woman I knew emailed me out of the blue one day in May. Her message sounded very cryptic:

How do you feel about Italy in July?

What on earth was she getting at? Couldn't she tell by my mercurial Facebook statuses like "FML: JUST GOT LAID-OFF. WILL CAT-SIT FOR CASH" and "I'M FREE!" that I wasn't in a great place emotionally or financially? I responded as any newly laid-off person would who is trying to stay bright and cheery rather than despondent and mortified.

I feel great about Italy in July, but I just got laid-off so . . . that's not happening for a while haha! But I think the layoff is for the best. I'll find something better. I'm pretty sure. Hopefully. Let me know if you hear of any jobs. I'll take pretty much anything. Anyway, about Italy . . . why do you ask?

I had to add the "Why do you ask?" just in case this woman I barely knew was about to offer me a free trip to Florence. You can lay a girl off, but you cannot take away her rich and wild imagination. Turns out that this woman was "seeing an Italian guy," and they were going to spend part of July sailing around on his boat.

"He has a friend who is single so I thought you might want to come along! You won't have to pay for a thing once we're there. No expectations, of course." Of course. Sailing around the Mediterranean without a care in the world sounded better than babysitting and combing Craigslist for entry-level jobs that had nothing to do with my chosen field. Plus, what if this "no expectations" guy was an Italian Ewan McGregor? What if he had a Six-Pack and was a Good Kisser? What if he were rich?

I tilted my head back, and my eyes floated to the ceiling as if it were a magical movie screen in the sky, and I imagined what it would be like to just take off and be one of those bikini-clad girls on a yacht. The pretend Italian sun felt amazing and my imaginary Prosecco was simply divine. I also had zero cellulite as I traipsed around in my bikini. It was all so tempting . . . Then the words "no expectations" popped into my head. The fact that she'd written "no expectations" led me to believe there would be expectations, and so my grand fantasy cut to black. Instead of staring at Italian Ewan McGregor, I was staring at Gmail.

"Sounds amazing, but I just can't. Thanks for asking though and have fun."

Maybe I was a big dumb baby and I should have splurged on a ticket and had a sexy gelato-fueled adventure. I've known men and women who have had a sugar mama or sugar daddy at some point in their life, and they're not riddled with syphilis and guilt. If this surprises you, please remember that I live in Los Angeles. It's so tempting to imagine being taken care of like royalty. Melanie was right—I didn't know what it was like to grow up with nothing. I went to summer camp, owned a Swatch, and had plenty of Barbie dolls. I even gave a buzz cut to the one cheap brunette knockoff Barbie we owned, named her Miss Dawn, and turned her into the "mean one," while all the legit Barbies with long blonde hair that my sisters and I named Kelly and Emily were sweet and popular. They all hated Miss Dawn since she was like a gruff drill sergeant and she was made of cheaper plastic, and the Kellys and Emilys went out of their way to exclude her. Looking back, I realize that this is regrettable behavior in more ways than one and I'm sorry.

I'm not sorry that I didn't go on that Italian vacation though. OK, maybe I'm a little sorry. But what's done is done, and I can buy my own Prosecco and gelato, thank you very much. It's usually from Trader Joe's, where the luxury items are reasonably priced. Maybe that's not as sexy as the Mediterranean vacation I could have had, but it beats having to kiss a sugar granddaddy or a random rich dude obsessed with wealth. No amount of gourmet gelato could sweeten that scenario. Even Melanie figured that out, and she was on the verge of having her tuition paid.

50

WHEN TO GO FOR BROKE

A lot of things went right over my head when I saw the movie *Grease* as a little kid. Rizzo's pregnancy scare? I just figured scowling was her thing. When she says to Danny, "Where are you goin'? To flog your log," I assumed that one of Danny's chores at home was to chop wood for his parents. And what were Sandy and Danny singing about at the end of the movie? "Wa baba lupop," or whatever they were saying, sounded fine way back when, but now it makes them sound like they're a little psycho. They hop into a car and levitate toward the clouds as they're belting out, "Sha na dipity boom," or whatever. As a five-year-old, to me the rhapsodic finale seemed totally plausible, like something I'd like to achieve in life. They were singing and dancing. They both, at the exact same time, pledged to always be together, along with all their high school friends. What could possibly go wrong from there?

Watching the movie as an adult is a totally different experience. You get pissed when it dawns on you that Rizzo is the constant target of 1950s slut shaming, and when you watch Sandy and Danny take off into the stratosphere, you think, "This is bullshit . . . why can't love be as simple as a musical?"

Because relationships are hard, that's why. And shiny red

convertibles don't just lift off and fly into the air unless you're dating Richard Branson and he can afford to have NASA build one for you.

Back in the *Grease* era, when I was prone to wearing Wonder Woman Underoos and singing into a hairbrush microphone, imitating my idol Olivia Newton-John, I wasn't imagining a kind, successful banker with a nest egg as I reached my hands to the heavens and warbled the lyrics to "Hopelessly Devoted to You."

My true-love's career wasn't part of the equation—being a T-Bird with a dimpled chin sounded promising enough. At that age, the profession of the object of your affection should not be a factor. It would have been demented if my sisters and I had sat around in pigtails combing through issues of *Forbes* and *Fortune*.

To remember a time when money played no role in my relationships, we'd have to go way back to one of my first loves (though not as far back as Ray Espinoza and ballsy Bobby Blair, who gave me a dyed-blue rose one day in kindergarten, which I rejected, like a diva). His name was Jim Doucet. Brown-eyed, 6'2" Jim. We were fourteen and I knew the instant I saw him saunter into Social Studies class that he was my Danny Zuko. He'd dyed the tips of his black hair fire-engine red; he wore black combat boots and a beat-up, safety-pin riddled black leather jacket with SEX PISTOLS across the back, and everyone was scared of him. The Perfect Man! Add that to the love list next to the all-important SIX-PACK: PEOPLE FEAR HIM. I didn't fear him though—his eyes were too pretty. One day, Jim slipped me a very romantic note written in red pencil:

Will you go with me?
☐ *Yes*   ☐ *No*

My heart exploded and I checked YES.

We were in eighth grade and we fell crazy in love. This wasn't "puppy love." I know it was real because our song was The Smiths's "There Is a Light That Never Goes Out." If you've never experienced the sheer emotion of this song, Morrissey sings about how heavenly it would be to get run over by a double decker bus, as long as his lover is by his side and they both go down together.

I really would have happily gotten smashed to oblivion by a double-decker bus if Jim were by my side and we could wind up on the side of the highway in a graceful, bittersweet, nonviolent tableau like Romeo and Juliet. I was becoming Sandy Olsen, only instead of flying into the sky in a convertible, my Zuko and I were being flattened into the cement by an eighteen-wheeler. Rational people might dream that their great romance will end like it did in *The Notebook*. Two well-dressed elderly people cuddled in bed passing away quietly in their sleep, with no eighteen-wheelers in sight. Where's the drama in that though?

Jim and I stayed together for two wildly romantic years. At night, we snuck away from our houses and met in the bayou behind my neighborhood, since all the PTA moms had convinced my parents that Jim was a horrible, scary drug dealer, thus making our romance a forbidden one, which of course only encouraged us and made it all the more glamorous. We talked on the phone all night until we both fell asleep. One winter day, we even lay on our backs in the bayou and spoke of whimsical things like the shapes of the clouds and the names of our future children. We were living our lives as if we were in a dreamy European movie, when really we were in the suburbs of Houston, Texas. Let me tell you, that takes a colossal amount of imagination to pull off.

But our romance wasn't always easy. A few months after that fateful day when I checked the YES box, Jim moved and enrolled in the performing arts school across town. Once he left, our love affair got a little pricier since we couldn't just eye-fuck each other in Social Studies anymore. Taxicabs were involved. Taxis and many winter days spent convincing my parents that I was staying late at school painting trompe l'oeil marble columns for our school's production of *Into the Woods*.

I did paint marble columns for the thespians, but only for an hour a day, Monday through Wednesday. My parents thought I was painting three hours a day, five days a week, which gave me tons of time to see my cross-town man. We split the cab fare, or Jim took the bus, so it wasn't so pricey. We even went to a movie once, but that was about the extent of our spending. At that age you're perfectly content listening to Morrissey and staring at each other until your chest aches and your heart implodes. We talked about our future, which involved marriage, children, and a cottage in England. Just talking about all of this entertained us for countless hours. I never once thought, "It's been a year already, and if this bum doesn't stop yapping about Sid Vicious and take me out to dinner just once I'm out of here." Show me an eighth-grader who demands that their boyfriend or girlfriend take them to a nice prix fixe and I'll show you high-maintenance demon spawn—most likely the love child of a Rich Kid of Instagram and a contestant on *The Bachelor*. Shows and websites like that make people think that dates equal sipping champagne in a French castle or having dinner onstage at the Hollywood Bowl, which is about as likely as getting to fly into the sky in a souped-up vintage Ford.

Where did this expectation for people to wine and dine each other come from? Was a caveman dragging in a bludgeoned deer as titillating to the cavewoman (or caveman) as a reservation at the French Laundry is to us? Most of us don't expect helicopter rides and oysters, but it sure is impressive and it does make you feel giddy. At least, I imagine it would. I've never been in a helicopter, but I have eaten oysters. In high school you don't really go out to dinner, unless it's out to the local Hunan Emperor for your pre-prom meal. I remember our greasy Chinese meal, and all of us in suits and colorful shiny dresses feeling very fancy and decadent and adult.

It makes us feel good to have things done for us, and bought for us. Somewhere along the line, this can go from being a nice surprise (like Jim buying my ticket to the movie theater) to a basic expectation, like hoping that your date has a full-time job with benefits and does not consider a mattress on the floor a bed. That's perfectly fine and normal, as long as we keep our expectations about love and money in perspective. Andrew Oswald, a British economics professor who interviewed over 6,000 couples about love and money, has said, "It is not low income that does most of the damage. It is dashed aspirations."[23]

There's a lot of pressure on both men and women when it comes to love and finances. Maybe it's OK that Sandy hops into the magical flying car with Danny Zuko. What kind of person would she be if she stood outside the convertible as the music soared and was like, "Well, where are you taking me? St. Tropez? And I want a tiara—a real one. And you need to get a real job because I am not marrying a mechanic!"

She'd be a real asshole, basically. Danny is a gifted mechanic (I think), and if Sandy marries him, she doesn't have to stress about finances if someone starts knocking the side mirror off her car with a baseball bat since I'm sure he'd be able to stick it back on. We never get to that part of the story though. The romantic movies never show us what happens after the car flies away or the plane takes off. In *Say Anything*, Diane Court (Ione Skye) and Lloyd Dobler (John Cusack) take off to England together so she can do her big-time fellowship and he can . . . kickbox. Lloyd is incredibly sweet, and he moves glass away in the street so she won't step on it and of course there's that whole jam box scene, but the first time he meets Diane's dad, he gives that speech about not wanting to buy anything processed or sell anything bought or processed, or process anything sold or bought. Basically Lloyd is saying he doesn't want to work in a cubicle for The Man.

I loved that speech in my teens, but now it's like, Lloyd needs to get a grip and figure his shit out, or else Diane is going to hook up with a posh Oxford law student who has his priorities in line. You may think I'm jaded, but I think I'm just more mature and practical. Why couldn't Lloyd have just said, "I want to kickbox for a living, and that is my plan, sir." Because he was eighteen, that's why. And he was just trying to figure it all out, like we all are.

23. "Andrew Oswald: For richer, for poorer" Accountancy Live September 2002 by Andrew Oswald https://www.accountancylive.com/andrew-oswald-richer-poorer

It's not that Sandy and Danny shouldn't have levitated into the sky at the end of *Grease*. No one wants to see the version where they're beaten down by life, living in Kenickie's basement, struggling to raise four kids, and bickering all the time. That doesn't mean we can't give their Hollywood ending a real-life, money-sucks, love-doesn't-conquer-all spin. Let's imagine that they're living in the real world—but we'll still allow the car to fly because if we didn't, then that would be pretty nihilistic, and it's good to have a little hope and belief that things will get better when dealing with love, life, floating convertibles, and money.

So, Danny and Sandy are in the flying car, singing . . .

Sandy: *Danny?*

Danny: *Babe! Ba-be-be-ba-di-be-di-bop!*

Sandy: *Danny. Can we stop singing and get serious for a second?*

Danny: *Yeah. OK. About what?*

Sandy: *I'm having a really great time, but . . . where exactly are we going?*

Danny: *Uh. That's a good point. I was just cruising.*

Sandy: *And we need to fill this thing up with gas at some point, right? I have $5.16. What about you?*

Danny: *$8.73. You're right—we're low on gas.*

Sandy: *Also, I never told you this but I want to go to law school.*

Danny: *Holy shit, babe. That's expensive. Like corporate law or something? Litigation?*

Sandy: *Civil rights.*

Danny: *Oh. That's a little less lucrative, I think.*

Sandy: *Yeah, I know. But it's my passion.*

Danny: *That's cool, that's cool. We'll make it work. Also, since we're talking, I thought Kenicke could live with us, 'til he gets on his feet.*

Sandy: *Oh hell no.*

Danny: *I like this feisty side of you.*

Sandy: *Me too. OK. So, we have $13.89 between us, no place to live, school loans to think about, and we're in a flying car. They didn't tell us about this part. We can't just fly around forever. Where's the script!? Where's the script!?*

Danny: *Deep breaths, babe. You want to get out?*

Sandy: *Do you?*

Danny: *Well, babe. I'm scared as shit, but no.*

Sandy: *OK. Me neither.*

Danny: *We're in it.*

Sandy: *That's true. We are.*

Danny: *Let's see what happens then?*

Sandy: *OK. Let's see what happens. But we need to get gas first. And figure out how to get more money. But one thing at a time, right?*

Danny: *Right. You got it. Hang on.*

INDEX

ACKNOWLEDGMENTS

First I want to thank my family for being so incredibly supportive and encouraging over the years. Thank you Mom for telling me early on, "Write whatever you want about me – look how Chelsea Handler talks about her mom!" Giving me the go-ahead to say whatever I please about you has been a true gift. Thank you for freeing me from a lifetime of guilt and shame. You're the best.

And to my dad, thank you for encouraging me even when I was trying to make a living babysitting and blogging for a lamp store and you were hoping I'd switch careers and go into Human Resources (interesting choice) or phlebotomy (even though the word "blood" makes me want to faint). You're also the best.

Thank you to my three amazing sisters for reminding me that there are always three phone calls I can make, no matter what.

A big shout out to my sweet granddad Big Papa - I hope you're reading this with a martini in hand.

Thank you to my friends (you know who you are – I hope) for keeping me sane when I contemplated trying out for The Bachelor or selling my hubcaps for cash. Thank you for letting me live on your couch, cry on your shoulder, and send you creative emoji combinations during the tough times.

And thank you to Jerett (aka JZ), who is the most wonderful man I've ever met, even though he has a rare medical condition in which ESPN seems to cancel out the frequency of my voice.

A big, huge, gigantic thank you to my amazing agent Brandi Bowles for believing in me, for being opinionated and supportive, and for working with me to develop this idea from the start. I could not have done it without your insight, intelligence, humor, and honesty.

Thank you to everyone at Seal Press for being so incredible to work with during this process. To my editor Stephanie Knapp for patiently answering my many, many emails with the subject line, "Me again!" Thank you for pushing me, for your smart, spot-on observations, and for everything you brought to this book.

Thank you to Kirsten, who showed me that the copyediting process could actually be fun, instead of excruciating, painful, and sad.

Thank you to everyone who read, shared, and supported my blog Bureaucracy for Breakfast. You guys gave me the guts to keep going.

I also wish to thank the National Association for the Advancement of Colored People for authorizing the use of Dorothy Parker's work, the Ava Gardner Trust for allowing me to use my favorite Ava Gardner quote, and my guru-with-a-pouf Nicole "Snooki" Polizzi for allowing me to use the quote that helped me survive a layoff.

And, last but not least, thank you to "Stan the MFA-phobe" for kicking me out of the cubicle and into the unknown.

ABOUT THE AUTHOR

Dina Gachman's comedic blog about the economy, Bureaucracy for Breakfast, has been featured on Marketplace on NPR and ABC's 20/20. Her writing has appeared in Forbes, Salon, The Hairpin, and Bustle, and she's written two comic books, about Marilyn Monroe and Elizabeth Taylor. She was born and raised in Texas, and she lives and writes in Los Angeles.

SELECTED TITLES FROM SEAL PRESS

For more than thirty years, Seal Press has published groundbreaking books. By women. For women.

Crap Job: How to Make the Most of the Job You Hate, by Michelle Goodman. $15.00, 978-1-58005-553-6. For the unhappily employed, author Michelle Goodman offers creative coping strategies and practical advice for surviving the workday along with much-needed comic relief.

The Anti 9-to-5 Guide: Practical Career Advice for Women Who Think Outside the Cube, by Michelle Goodman. $14.95, 978-1-58005-186-6. Escape the wage-slave trap of your cubicle with Goodman's hip career advice on creating your dream job and navigating the work world without compromising your aspirations.

My So-Called Freelance Life: How to Survive and Thrive as a Creative Professional for Hire, by Michelle Goodman. $15.95, 978-1-58005-259-7. From the author of *The Anti 9-to-5 Guide*, this how-to guidebook offers invaluable tips and first-hand advice to help women turn their freelance dreams into reality.

Spent: Exposing Our Complicated Relationship with Shopping, edited by Kerry Cohen. $17.00, 978-1-58005-512-3. Women reveal the impact that spending money has on their emotions, their self-worth, and their relationships.

What You Can When You Can: 50 Ways to Reach Your Healthy Living Goals, by Carla Birnberg and Roni Noone. $10.00, 978-1-58005-573-4. This companion book to the #wycwyc movement teaches you to harness the power of small steps to achieve your health and fitness goals.

Screw Everyone: Sleeping My Way to Monogamy, by Ophira Eisenberg. $16.00, 978-1-58005-439-3. Comedian Ophira Eisenberg's wisecracking account of how she spent most of her life saying "yes" to everything—and everyone—and how that attitude ultimately helped her overcome her phobia of commitment.

Find Seal Press Online
www.sealpress.com
www.facebook.com/sealpress
Twitter: @SealPress